SCHOOLS
for CITIES

ORGANISATION FOR CO-OPERATION AND ECONOMIC DEVELOPMENT

ORGANISATION FOR ECONOMIC CO-OPERATION AND DEVELOPMENT

Pursuant to Article 1 of the Convention signed in Paris on 14th December 1960, and which came into force on 30th September 1961, the Organisation for Economic Co-operation and Development (OECD) shall promote policies designed:

— to achieve the highest sustainable economic growth and employment and a rising standard of living in Member countries, while maintaining financial stability, and thus to contribute to the development of the world economy;

— to contribute to sound economic expansion in Member as well as non-member countries in the process of economic development; and

— to contribute to the expansion of world trade on a multilateral, non-discriminatory basis in accordance with international obligations.

The original Member countries of the OECD are Austria, Belgium, Canada, Denmark, France, Germany, Greece, Iceland, Ireland, Italy, Luxembourg, the Netherlands, Norway, Portugal, Spain, Sweden, Switzerland, Turkey, the United Kingdom and the United States. The following countries became Members subsequently through accession at the dates indicated hereafter: Japan (28th April 1964), Finland (28th January 1969), Australia (7th June 1971), New Zealand (29th May 1973) and Mexico (18th May 1994). The Commission of the European Communities takes part in the work of the OECD (Article 13 of the OECD Convention).

Publié en français sous le titre :
L'ÉCOLE DANS LA VILLE

THE PROGRAMME ON EDUCATIONAL BUILDING

PEB

PEB promotes the international exchange of ideas, information, research and experience in the field of educational facilities. For more than 20 years, it has worked to ensure that the maximum educational benefit is obtained from past and future investment, so that buildings and equipment are designed effectively as well as planned and managed efficiently.

The three main themes of the programme's work are:

● improving the quality and suitability of educational facilities and thus contributing to the quality of education;

● ensuring that the best possible use is made of the very substantial sums of money which are spent on constructing, running and maintaining educational facilities; and

● giving early warning of the impact on educational facilities of trends in education and in society as a whole.

The report which follows was inspired by a conference on 'Renewing urban schools', organised by the OECD Programme on Educational Building in conjunction with the State of Maryland, and which was held in Baltimore in 1992. It draws on and continues some of the conclusions reached at that conference, and relates them to changes which are taking place in society. It is illustrated both with reference to experiences which were presented on that occasion, and also to many others drawn primarily from the United Kingdom and the United States. Conceived and created by Mike Duckenfield, Consultant to the Programme on Educational Building (PEB), the report should be seen as a personal view of developments which are taking place. It is intended to stimulate debate about the role – potential and actual – of educational facilities in the life and development of towns and cities.

The report is published on the responsibility of the Secretary General of the OECD but its views do not engage any of the Member governments.

Mike Duckenfield has written about education for many publications in several countries. In the 1970s he was Scandinavia Correspondent of The Times Educational Supplements (London). During the 1980s, he covered higher education, continuing education and training, in the press office of the UK Department of Education and Science. He is a member of the DSM Partnership, a research and information consultancy specialising in education and economic development issues.

3

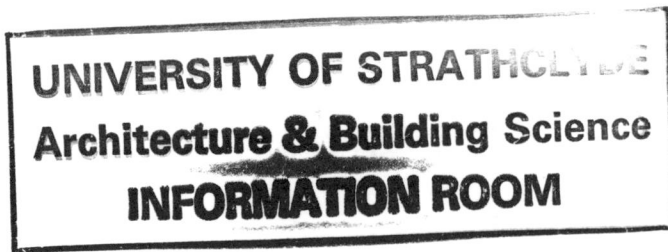

ACKNOWLEDGEMENTS

In writing this book, I called upon many voices to supplement my own. Also, I received information or other assistance from several others. However, the arguments presented are mine alone. I should like to thank the following:

Gregor Friedl, ZNWB, Berlin, Germany; Martin Garden, Lothian Regional Council, Edinburgh, Scotland; Michael Hacker, consultant, London, England; Warren Hathaway, Alberta Education, Edmonton, Canada; Manfred Hinum, Ministry of Education and Art, Vienna, Austria; Christian Kallerdahl, Department of Education, Gothenburg, Sweden; Amy Linden, New York City Board of Education, New York, USA; John Mayfield and Tamsyn Alley, MFP-Adelaide, Australia; Edward McMilin, Milwaukee Public Schools, Milwaukee, USA; Christiane Nicolas, Mayor's Office, and Henri-Antoine Millers, Technical Services Buildings Division 1, Lyon, France; Graham Parker, Beech Williamson, Sophie Jackson and Andy Thompson, Architects and Building Division, Department for Education, London, England; Yvonne Plows, CTC Trust Ltd., London, England; Kees Roos and Martin Walop, Crime Prevention Office, Haarlem City Council, Netherlands; Barbara Sakellariou-Rigas and Nassie Xanalatou, Ministry of National Education and Religion, Athens, Greece; Malcolm Skilbeck, OECD; Paul Stirner, DSM Partnership, London, England; Susan Stuebing, New Jersey Institute of Technology, Newark, USA; Teun van Wijk, ICS, Gouda, Netherlands; and Richard Yelland, OECD/PEB.

Throughout the text, unless otherwise stated, all financial figures are expressed in terms of US dollars.

Mike Duckenfield

Easter 1994

CONTENTS

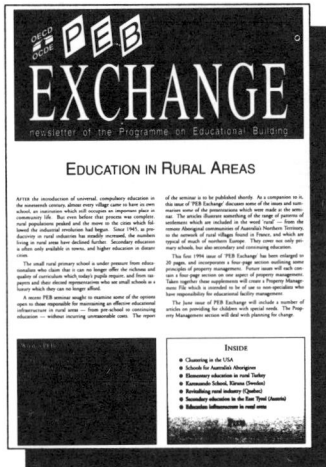

INTRODUCTION

In the summer of 1992 the OECD's Programme on Educational Building, in conjunction with the State of Maryland, held a seminar on school and college facilities and urban renewal, in Baltimore, and I was asked to be the rapporteur. Much interesting and useful information was presented which, in an extended, revised and updated form, provides the basis for the case studies in this publication. However, I came away from the event thinking that a framework was needed into which these apparently disparate examples could be fitted. Moreover, it should be one which offered a positive and practical view of urban development – one that stressed possibilities rather than problems.

I settled on the question: 'How does education contribute to the prosperity of cities and those who live in them?' – and this was the starting point for the essay. In summary, I argue that education has an important supporting role in economic development – by contributing to the physical environment, fostering social interaction, and imparting the knowledge and skills needed for work. But education can also take steps to deal with problems arising from social conditions, and other circumstances, found in cities; and it has a function in creating a climate favourable to innovation and adaptability to change – particularly significant when cities, education itself, and society are experiencing an era of transformation.

The first chapter of the essay concludes by saying that we need a vision of a 'learning city' of the 21st century, which takes these factors into account. The second focuses on six themes which illustrate the connections between education and aspects of economic development, and the third looks at three of the social contexts for education – families and poverty, race and ethnicity, and crime. Finally, the fourth chapter deals with planning issues in creating the learning city – implementing change, innovation, and the need for partnership. In particular, it discusses the role of, and states the case for, government.

The canvas is broad, and deliberately so – for two reasons. First, I wanted to take the planning, design and management of education facilities – buildings, equipment, grounds – out of the professional 'ghetto' of facilities specialists and show that the issues concerned have relevance for, and deserve the attention of, a much wider audience. Second, as I hope the text makes clear, the notion of a learning city implies an holistic approach: its creation involves the weaving together of many strands, by many people and organisations.

This publication provides a survey, based on extensive desk research. Experience has been gathered from more than a dozen OECD countries, with examples in the text featuring over 40 cities. Nonetheless, there is an unmistakable Anglo-

American bias. Two-thirds of the examples are drawn from the United States and the United Kingdom, and much of the discussion centres on developments perhaps more typically found in these countries than in other OECD countries.

Some readers may feel that examples drawn from the USA, in particular, are too specifically American to allow wider application. I disagree. With three exceptions, urban trends in the United States are mirrored in cities elsewhere, albeit in a reduced form. Besides, the USA is probably unrivalled in the extent of its innovation in education and the degree to which it evaluates its experiments, providing insights not always easily obtainable elsewhere. (What does make the USA distinctive are: the proliferation of firearms; the lack of a comprehensive welfare safety net; and the weakness, and hence unreformability, of its government. Race, which might have been included a generation ago, is not in the list: themes of dispossession and exclusion, and of integration, apply to racial and ethnic minorities in cities throughout the industrialised world.)

Mike Duckenfield

Easter 1994

1968

To raise the level of urban education across the board will require money; but money is not enough. We will need teachers; but teachers are not enough. We will need research, and educational research is already giving us new teaching techniques, new methods of evaluating academic progress, and a host of additional aids in educating the slum child. But research is not enough.

What is enough?

Perhaps the answer to that question will emerge only when every American recognizes that educating the slum child as a way of breaking the chain of poverty is in his own immediate, direct interest. For this is one of the lessons that your city and all the cities of the United States teach: that our well-being, our safety, the very quality of our lives and those of our children are bound up with the lives of countless other men whom we will never know and may never see.

Harold Halt, *The Schoolhouse in the City*.[1]

1991

My deepest impression was simply that urban schools were, by and large, extraordinarily unhappy places. With few exceptions, they reminded me of 'garrisons' or 'outposts' in a foreign nation.

Housing projects, bleak and tall, surrounded by perimeter walls lined with barbed wire, often stood adjacent to the schools I visited.

The schools were surrounded frequently by signs that indicated DRUG-FREE ZONE. Their doors were guarded. Police sometimes patrolled the halls. The windows of the schools were often covered with steel grates. Taxi drivers flatly refused to take me to some of these schools...

Looking around some of these inner-city schools, where filth and disrepair were worse than anything I'd seen in 1964, I often wondered why we agree to let our children go to school in places where no politician, school board president, or business CEO would dream of working. Children seem to wrestle with these kinds of questions too. Some of their observations were, indeed, so trenchant that a teacher sometimes would step back and raise her eyebrows and then nod at me across the children's heads, as if to say, 'Well, there it is! They know what's going on around them, don't they?'

Jonathan Kozol, *Savage Inequalities*.[2]

I

Education and Urban Prosperity

The physical problems are obvious: deteriorating schools; ageing infrastructure; a diminishing manufacturing base; a health care system, short of doctors, that fails to immunize against measles, much less educate about AIDS. The jobs have disappeared. The neighborhoods have been gutted. A genuine depression has hit the cities – unemployment, in some areas, matches the levels of the 1930s. **Senator Bill Bradley, of New Jersey, speaking in the US Senate, March 1992.**[3]

When you fail to educate children, particularly poor children... You generate another generation of people who become tax consumers instead of tax producers. **Ted Kimbrough, superintendent, Chicago public schools.**[4]

IT IS AN ODD REVERSAL OF EXPERIENCE THAT RURAL LIFE, SO OFTEN MEAN AND harsh, has come to be depicted in an Edenic glow whereas cities, which have bestowed on humankind the most obvious benefits and pleasures of civilisation, frequently invoke the language of apocalypse.

However, it is not in the nature of cities to be safe or comfortable: it is not why they thrive. Different from rural areas and small towns, cities are dynamic and progressive. They offer personal freedom and the prospect of economic betterment, and they succeed in this by providing endless opportunities for people who had been strangers to meet each other and to profit by the experience. Such connections make the spark of enterprise, whether these new ventures be commercial or philanthropic, recreational or vocational, public or domestic, or even legal or illegal.

Nor is the path of urban fortunes smooth, as the uneven accretion of architectural styles that marks successive property booms bears witness; and to these cyclical fluctuations, too, we should be wary of over-reacting. As Simon

Jenkins, the former editor of *The Times*, concluded in the 1992 annual London Lecture: "In the life of cities there is no crisis, only that oldest of cycles, birth and rebirth... As long as the city can keep open the arteries of its economy, it can recover."[5]

On several scores, though, history may no longer be a reliable guide: cities are changing in unprecedented ways, with outcomes which cannot be securely predicted.

Urban dynamics

By transforming movement within cities, mass motor transport, initially, and more recently telecommunications technology have fundamentally altered the way people and organisations carry out their daily transactions. As a result, notions of urban proximity are being redefined. Functions once carried out in neighbourhoods or downtown may now be performed 'somewhere in the suburbs' or beyond. Offices, banks and hotels that once felt obliged to cluster physically realise they can equally well carry out their business almost regardless of location. An increasing number of people are working from home.

▷ UNITED STATES

In the United States, where dispersal is most pronounced, there were in 1950 only about 100 purpose-built suburban shopping centres. By 1960, there were 6 700, including the first of the enclosed 'malls'. At the end of 1992, there were nearly 39 000 malls, including 1 835 defined as 'regional malls', comprising more than 400 000 square feet (37 160 sq. metres) of retail space. Not merely places in which to shop, they house entertainment complexes, restaurants and, increasingly, government offices and even schools. Similarly, by moving to the urban periphery, companies have found that they can cut costs and offer a better living environment to their employees without any apparent commercial ill-effect.

In spite of talk of urban consolidation to reduce traffic congestion and pollution, the bonds that hold cities together are loosening. From being centripetal, many cities are projecting outwards and becoming multi-centred, with several, sometimes rival, nodes of commercial development. Whether the motive on the part of inhabitants is to escape the high costs of 'in-town' living, as in cities such as Paris and Tokyo, or to flee socially-deprived and 'problem-ridden' inner city districts, as in the United States, the move to suburbs and ex-urban communities is a choice made increasingly feasible by modern communications.

▷ DETROIT

But new technology can also be used to foster social cohesion – between neighbourhoods, races and even nations. 'Connections' is a collaboration between Highland Park Commmunity High School in a poor and predominantly African-American municipality within the boundaries of Detroit and Grosse Ile High School, 30 miles away in an affluent and mostly white community on an island in the Detroit River, facing Canada.

Taking advantage of (Michigan) state technology grants, which paid for computers, fax machines, phone lines, access to databases, on-line computer time and teacher training, staff developed a history unit that could be accommodated into the curriculum of both schools. Students are given assignments which they have to complete jointly; mixed-school teams carry out larger projects; and there is a common test at the end of the unit. Reinforcing these links are joint field trips, which include collaborative team-building exercises, and an annual day-long discussion and work session which alternates between the schools. Recently, two more schools have joined the scheme – in Latino and Arab-American communities in the Detroit area.

What pattern are cities likely to assume in future? Where should urban facilities be located, and how can they and their users be 'connected'? How should we deal with the problem of unprosperous districts, by applying 'intensive care' and trying to restore to them their traditional purposes (for example, by creating enterprise zones), or by revitalising them with new functions – as theme parks, urban villages or campuses for education, training and research?

Urban growth

Whether by suburbanisation, the creation of 'edge cities'[6] or the 'colonisation' of nearby towns, or all three, the area and orbit of major urban centres has extended considerably and will continue to grow. Discussion of the urban future in terms of cities, therefore, is becoming increasingly irrelevant. As a recent OECD publication points out, three-quarters of the people in the OECD's member countries live in cities, and "many developed countries are now entering, or have already entered, an era when... the actual area occupied by urban growth will rival that devoted to cultivation".[7]

However, official city population statistics obscure this growth. Indeed, they often suggest that populations are declining. Greater London has 6.7 million inhabitants but the contiguous urban area of which it forms the centre has 10.4 million, and similar differences exist for many other cities, including Paris, Milan and Madrid. In the United States, the 1990 census found that, for the first time, a majority of Americans live in cities of more than a million inhabitants. The sprawling Los Angeles megalopolis contained 14.5 million people – almost half of California's population, and 3.3 million more than in 1980 – and the New York 'region' was home to 18.1 million.

How do we plan for urban prosperity when the political jurisdictions of city government no longer encompass the 'economic city'? How can public resources be used equitably and efficiently in the urban area as a whole? How do you overcome local political obstacles to achieve co-ordinated planning in relation to factors affecting economic development, including the creation of physical infrastructure and education and training?

The OECD report went on to warn: "... cities have reached dimensions that change the very terms of the relationship between development and urbanisation. ...development may be slowed or even stopped by unorganised urban growth. Local authorities and governments unable to cope with urban problems will be responsible for the consequent lack of development or even for the decline of their economies."

Global cities

Never before have so many people, in so many countries, lived and worked in a country other than that in which they or their parents were born. In consequence, cities – where all but a few migrants settle – are becoming intrinsically multiracial and ethnically diverse.

The United Nations estimated that, in 1993, 100 million people – almost one in fifty of the world's population – were living outside their native country, double the number in 1990.

Since the 1950s, cities in Europe, and those founded by Europeans elsewhere, have progressively lost their ethnic homogeneity. In 1950, no major American city had more than a 40 per cent 'black' population. In 1990, 20 cities did, and in half African-Americans comprised a majority. One in four Australians is now born into a home where the first language is other than English; between one in ten and one in twenty residents in France's three largest cities is North African; in the Netherlands nearly 400 (of 8 000) schools have majority 'ethnic' enrolments (primarily of Surinamese, Turks, Moroccans, and Antilleans); and almost half the inner city population of Britain's second largest city, Birmingham belongs to a 'non-white' ethnic group.

Is 'the melting pot' possible – or desirable? How do you balance the need for common values against 'respect for difference'? Can democratic institutions empower minorities? What is the place of the established culture, including language and religion? What must be done to bring often poorly, and badly, educated minorities 'up to speed' in advanced economies? How can education be more effective as an agent for social mobility?

Richard Weinstein, an urban affairs specialist at the University of California, Los Angeles, believes: "The multi-ethnic factor in governance and politics in big urban centers is going to be the central issue for the future, and one that we are unprepared to deal with. The difficulty of talking across cultures and across languages and across traditions – the kinds of things that have divided nation-states for centuries – are to some degree being miniaturized within our cities."[8]

Urban regeneration

Meeting the challenges posed by urban change presents a formidable task. Not all cities have the economic diversity to 'bounce back': some that grew around a single industry or function – such as textile and steel towns, mining communities, and ports – may face an historic reduction in their size and importance. More usually, however, urban crisis focuses on particular districts which are depressed in relation to the city as a whole. These are by no means all 'inner cities'; many are peripheral districts, often created in slum clearance programmes, which lack employment and have a high concentration of social disadvantage.

New and refurbished buildings, of themselves, do not constitute urban renewal, but are one of the many components in regeneration – the process which "seeks to reverse the vicious spiral in which physical, economic and social problems interface with each other".[9] The UK government, in support of its urban development programmes, has proposed six broad 'resource categories' to describe the conditions for sustained physical and economic improvement. These are location, finance, infrastructure, amenities, human aspects, and a category for 'intangibles' such as community cohesion, institutional capacity, and quality of life.

Within these categories are a number of factors which research has shown indicate potential for regeneration, several of which have, or many have, relevance for education. They include:

● the presence of research and development activity, for example through the creation of science and technology parks, and of higher education – as a focus for information, learning and research, and as an employer, property developer, and means to enhance the 'image' of a district;

● access to resources outside the district through the use of telecommunications links;

● the quality of the overall physical environment, including the absence of dereliction and poorly-maintained buildings and grounds;

● the availability of pre-school nursery places, as well as low teacher turnover and low levels of student truancy;

● access to medical and dental care, particularly for low-income families;

● the quality and range of educational facilities – "renowned as a factor used by many (potential) migrants to choose between alternative locations" and "a clear element in the different 'life chances' of young people in different areas";

● the presence of sport, entertainment and leisure facilities and activities, and a good level of participation in voluntary and community-based activities;

● a relatively low risk of experiencing crime;

● a good level of basic educational attainment and a culture that encourages enterprise (including by example, such as the presence of small businesses and the self-employed);

● the absence of 'spatial polarisation' between different social (and ethnic) groups; and

● the ability of government and others to work together in 'multi-agency' and 'integrated' approaches to meeting local needs.

The role of education

Perhaps the most important contribution education can make to the prosperity of cities and those who live in them, given movement within and between countries, is to provide citizens, both children and adults, with the knowledge, skills and other attributes so that they may thrive anywhere.

Thus, there is a universal requirement for adequate pre-school facilities and programmes to enable all young children to become 'ready for school'; schools which are effective in developing students cognitively and morally and in preparing them for work; and, beyond 'compulsory' schooling, easy access for adults of all ages to further study, training and retraining.

For education authorities this implies an expansion of pre-school places; changes in the organisation of teaching space and the modernisation of facilities to accommodate new learning methods, notably equipping schools for new information technologies; improved access to, and provision of, up-to-date equipment and environments for vocational education and training; and the creation of accessible and 'user-friendly' places for adult learning.

Education authorities can also take steps to deal with problems arising from social conditions, and other circumstances, which may have a high urban incidence and, though not unique to cities, may combine in ways that are distinctively 'urban'. Such problems often impinge on the work of schools and affect those who study and teach in them. Taking steps to alleviate their effects can benefit individuals educationally and help them to prosper in other ways. For example:

● After-school activities and youth recreation programmes provide an alternative for students to being 'home alone' and 'running on the streets', and may help reduce peer pressure to join gangs and engage in anti-social behaviour leading to crime. They may also reduce truancy and dropping out.

● Child-care facilities make it easier for women generally, and those dependent on welfare in particular, to enter employment. School-based 'return to learn' classes allow adults to gain qualifications to enhance their job prospects.

● The existence of school cafeterias and integrated welfare and nutrition education programmes can assist in ensuring that children of low-income households are adequately and properly fed. This helps children concentrate in class.

● Where there is an influx of immigrants, extra classes, and maybe special facilities, can help students overcome any deficiency in the normal language of tuition. Schools might also take a lead in providing language and social education classes for immigrant adults, one benefit being to enable parents to support their children in their schoolwork.

● Where poverty requires students to supplement family income, education authorities and individual schools could employ older students in minor repair, maintenance and cleaning, landscaping, and night cafeteria work. This would relieve pressure on students to drop out and provide a 'controlled' alternative to part-time employment in commercial jobs which detract from learning (due to their hours and conditions).

● The inclusion of health care services on 'school' premises may assist the diagnosis and treatment of students with substance abuse problems and support drugs education generally. It may also promote AIDS prevention and sexual responsibility and help reduce teenage pregnancy, and it can provide more effective ante- and post-natal care for student mothers.

The learning city

What is required if education is to contribute effectively to the prosperity of cities and those who live in them is an holistic approach, based on a vision of the kind of learning city that we shall need in the early 21st century. This vision should encompass the fundamentals of education provision, including:

● what is taught as part of basic schooling (that is, during the years of compulsory school attendance) and how opportunities for learning both before and after this period, and through life, are provided;

● how teaching and learning are effected pedagogically – through tuition, experiential learning, self-study, project work and experimentation – and what is needed to support this (mentoring, counselling, new means of assessment);

● where teaching and learning take place and 'means of access': in educational institutions, such as schools and colleges, at the workplace, in the community, and at home; by attendance or new methods of 'delivery' or both; and

● who pays for education and training; who is responsible for its provision; and who manages it.

17

And it should also embrace:

● the contribution of education to the overall urban 'knowledge infrastructure' and to the quality of the physical environment;

● its contribution to community development, and social integration and cohesion, and ways in which the social context of learning can be addressed; and

● the means by which an organisational culture favourable to innovation – responding to, and planning for, change as an opportunity – can be fostered, so as to meet these challenges.

Answers to the questions raised by these issues are crucial to the planning, design, management and use of educational facilities.

Building the Learning City

WE NOW TURN TO DISCUSSION OF A NUMBER OF TOPICS WHICH ILLUSTRATE SOME of the themes identified. Ways in which education can relate to three aspects of the social context of learning – family life, race, and crime – will be examined in the third section of this essay.

Investing to enhance the built environment

...the architectural profession has still, in what purports to be a truly democratic society, to come to terms with the practice of making buildings with people, rather than being content to design for them... architects need to re-discover the creative role of briefing and to develop new, more participatory, ways of working.
Richard Weston, *Schools of Thought.*[10]

Long range cost-effectiveness is critical. We must move beyond 'first cost', and consider costs over the lifetime of the facility.
Richard Hobbs, American Institute of Architects.[11]

New and renovated school buildings should always benefit the urban landscape, even if only because they replace ones that were decrepit and had become eyesores. They may be aesthetically pleasing, enhancing the 'character' of the neighbourhood, as well as 'environmentally-friendly', for example by promoting energy conservation. And, of course, they should be well-equipped and a great asset as a resource for learning and other activities.

However, the planning of new or improved facilities can also be seen as an opportunity to assist urban regeneration. The creation of the Centre of Knowledge at Lindholmen, as the centrepiece of a major redevelopment of Gothenburg's former docklands, is an example. On a more modest scale, renovation of a school in the English railway town of Crewe has been a catalyst for the creation of community recreation facilities and housing improvements, as well as influencing decisions regarding the design of a new shopping centre and an urban highway. (See case studies for details of both these examples.)

The benefits of linking the planning of educational facilities with community and wider urban developments work 'both ways'.

● 'Non-education' money, from within government and the private and voluntary sectors, can be attracted to support projects which include school improvements (and which might not be possible to finance without it), while joint planning may reduce the costs involved in carrying out developments separately.

● Social costs, too, may be reduced, by planning education improvements to accord with community needs. Thus, for example, neighbourhood crime prevention may be assisted as part of a scheme to reduce the vandalism of school buildings (see examples in the next section and the Haarlem case study).

● 'Trade-offs' are possible which result in a more varied physical infrastructure and one that promotes social interaction. On the one hand, new education facilities may include space for 'non-educational' purposes, such as a public library, a neighbourhood restaurant (perhaps run commercially as an enterprise project by students), a crèche, and rented or leased workshops for business start-ups. On the other, new facilities created 'in the community' (including the private sector) may be planned to include public educational uses, relating to adult education, for instance.

The key is a collaborative and co-ordinated approach to planning, and how this may be best achieved. It requires education authorities to work with a much wider range of people and organisations than they have been accustomed to do – not only within municipal government, neighbouring authorities and other levels of government, but in the private and voluntary sectors and the community itself – that is, those who live and work or run businesses there. There are several devices that have been used in such an approach, including specially-created public authorities, for example development corporations, 'one-off' partnerships and joint management schemes. The crucial question, however, is 'How do you organise so as to make consideration of potential benefits to the urban infrastructure a routine part of education facility planning?' One way might be to institute 'community opportunity appraisals', much the same as environmental impact analyses are now required.

Another, related consideration is that of educational buildings as property investment. Pick up a brochure proudly presenting the new schools built in many cities, states and other jurisdictions, look at the pictures and plans, and ask 'What use will this have in 2040? Will it still be suitable for education?

Can we convert it to other uses? Can it be sold?'

Adaptability and flexibility are key quality measures for educational facilities. As defined by the OECD Programme on Educational Building, the former concerns the possibility of large magnitude/ low frequency change, such as the "relocation, replacement, removal or addition of the constructional elements, the services, or the finishes of the building", while the latter, conversely, entails low magnitude/ high frequency change... "which permits variations in activities, timetabling, class size, and methods of work".[12]

Both involve a long-term view by planners, and an OECD report on adaptability and flexibility says education authorities should consider continuing costs ("life costs") in planning new facilities, rather than only initial capital and equipment costs. They should employ investment appraisal techniques to determine an appropriate cost target for a project – that is, to assess expenditure in the light of the likely future benefits to be gained from the investment.[13] (For a design of a new school with built-in adaptability, see the case study on New Leith Academy in Edinburgh.)

This investment will be more secure (and public money more wisely spent) if due consideration is also given to demographic and other trends. Take, for example, the problem of dealing with the rapid growth in school enrolments often characteristic of new suburbs. The usual solution is to erect mobile classrooms, partly due to the immediacy of needs, but also because authorities fear spending large sums on big schools and additions which may not be needed in a generation's time. "We used to build elementary schools right in the middle of new sub-divisions," says British Columbia education minister Douglas Hibbins. "It seemed to make logistical sense. Then the kids grew up, the neighborhood became 'middle-aged', and we were left with an under-used building in a poor location. We now seek to build schools on arterial roads, with better access to public transport, so that they can more readily be converted to other uses. And, it's easier to sell them, if we have to – and we get a better price."[14]

EDMONTON ◁

In the neighbouring province of Alberta, in the commuter city of St Albert, outside Edmonton, a prototype 'convertible school' has been built with the intention of later adaptation into 18 self-contained apartments for senior citizens. The inclusion of features in the design, facilitating conversion, raised initial costs by five per cent, but the province expects to more than recoup this by halving the construction costs that would normally be associated with creating the subsequent facility.

In a variation of this strategy, new houses in an Adelaide suburb have been bought, adapted, and leased to schools, with the intention of re-converting them back to residential use when the pressure on school places subsides. And, in

Sweden, this logic has been taken a step further. Instead of building 'schools', some cities are constructing multi-function facilities where space can be used flexibly to accommodate a variety of local services, including education, so that a school occupies as much as it requires, as needs change.

Overall, the best value for public expenditure can only be obtained if the planning and management of educational buildings is carried out within an authority-wide or institutional estate management strategy. In guidance to British colleges, the national agency responsible for the allocation of (public) funding specifies that such a strategy should include three elements within a general strategic plan, dealing with the college's mission.[15] These are an accommodation strategy, a maintenance investment plan (to "determine the type and extent of maintenance each building justifies within the accommodation strategy and the available resources"), and a plan for the funding and day-to-day control of maintenance.

The accommodation strategy should specify how property may be changed to fit the general strategic plan. It should be based on an evaluation of the existing estate, identify opportunities for development, examine the options and their financial implications (including through the use of investment appraisal), and include an assessment of space utilisation.

In considering development opportunities, the guidance says colleges should assess the value of their sites and buildings in terms of opportunity cost; that is, the maximum value which could be achieved if the property were put to an alternative use – for example, through sale or leasing. This should be weighed against the cost of replacing the facility "with property which would be more fundamentally suitable, more efficient in space utilisation, in better condition, in a more convenient location, cheaper, or which has... other advantages over the existing [facility], taking into account... repair costs and maintenance and running costs". In extreme cases, the best investment may involve complete relocation of the college – or school.

Modernising and improving school buildings

Our aim is to create a city where children are kings.
Michel Noir, mayor of Lyon.[16]

Do we have the imagination to envision the features of world-class schools for all the children of Manhattan?... The real test of progress will be to count how many inner-city schools have been turned into... world-class learning communities by the year 2000.
Arthur G. Wirth, *Education and Work for the Year 2000: Choices We Face*.[17]

School buildings usually have a long life, often much longer than originally intended. Most of the schools that the grandchildren of today's teenagers will attend have been built and are currently in use. Improving and maintaining the quality of existing facilities, therefore, is a major infrastructure task, and it has implications for educational achievement.

Poor educational environments do affect learning. Repairs due to breakdowns or vandalism result in lost classtime, and paying for them uses money that might be spent on teaching or materials. Access to equipment, certain rooms and even courses may be denied. Teacher morale and student pride can suffer. There is also some evidence connecting the quality of school facilities with test scores and student behaviour.[18]

The age of buildings is only one of the factors in determining the task of improving the physical infrastructure of schools. There is also the sheer size of the inventory and the fact that much of it has been allowed to run down due to budget squeezes and irregular maintenance. In many cities, the scale of the problem requires the impact of a major capital programme, to eliminate the backlog of repairs and adapt schools for new teaching and learning methods. One city doing this is France's second largest, Lyon (see case study).

By their nature, however, such programmes are 'one-offs', or at least can only be repeated occasionally. More often, an incremental approach will be needed, and this is more likely to be successful if it is part of a development plan (within an overall accommodation strategy). This enables small, self-contained steps to be taken as, and when, funds become available, not in a piecemeal way but progressively, with sight of an 'end goal'. Indeed, by making better use of existing resources, the case for funding may be more easily argued than it would be for a major replacement or renovation project.

Such a strategy should be flexible. As a recent report on upper secondary schools and colleges in Britain says: "There is a need for a development plan [to be] kept under continual review" – for architectural and educational reasons – "and for rigorous consideration of how to plan and finance change – capital bids, self-financing, and use of recurrent monies (making, for example, change of use or adaptation coincide with bringing buildings in poor shape up to standard and routine maintenance)."[19]

Whichever the approach adopted, the benefits of renovation will soon be dissipated if the condition of schools is not continuously monitored, repairs carried out, and adequate and dedicated funding made available for maintenance. In this, too, good management makes a difference. Some cities have shown that, by using new techniques and adopting long-term plans and minimum standards, progressive improvements can be achieved (see the case study on approaches to maintenance). Early evidence on school-based management in England suggests that school autonomy over operational budgets may benefit maintenance and repair.

As in Lyon, improvement must go hand-in-hand with modernisation: schools need to be remodelled and re-equipped to meet future needs, not merely be brought up to contemporary standards. Particular needs are for the widespread introduction and implementation of new technologies – computers, and cable and satellite links – and the creation of a greater diversity of working spaces than is catered for by the traditional classroom.

Some countries have made large strides in the provision of information technology. In the last four years, the ratio of students to computers in Japan has fallen from more than 400 to one to fewer than 50 in lower secondary schools (ages 12-15) and from more than 200 to 24 in high schools (ages 15-18). Britain, where former education minister Kenneth Baker recalls, in 1981, "over half our schools did not have any sort of computer",[20] had, by 1991/92, achieved ratios of 25:1 in primary schools (ages 5-11) and13:1 in secondary schools (ages 11-16/18).[21] However, as Norman Willis has pointed out in a recent OECD report, information technology will not be realised as a new means of learning until the limited access and uses implied by 'computer rooms' is replaced by a personal computer on the desk of every student and teacher.[22] (Regarding cable and satellite links, the United States is probably leading the field: only 6 615 schools were wired to receive cable television in 1989, but three years later this had increased to more than 60 000 schools, comprising 61 per cent of the total.)

Consideration must also be given to the rate at which buildings are expected to become too uneconomical to run, or grossly unsuited for their purpose, and thus need to be taken out of use; the rigorous elimination of surplus space (where it exists) can provide a 'head start', by removing some of the oldest and worst buildings.

Most fundamentally, the issue is not one of how to raise the overall quality of public school buildings but, rather, how to ensure good quality learning environments for all students. If the tactics referred to above – major capital programmes and incremental improvement, supported by maintenance, modernisation and selective closure of the least fit buildings – are thought unlikely to be sufficient, or feasible, urban school districts will need to consider abandoning buildings (and selling them and their sites), and moving some schools into rented or leased property.

Making more of educational facilities

...time is the uncracked nut. It's a prism through which we can look anew at teacher time, student motivation, and curriculum.
Milton Goldberg, executive director, US National Education Commission on Time and Learning.[23]

Administrative pigeonholing is perhaps the largest obstacle in... combining the school with other neighbourhood facilities.
Teun van Wijk, consultant to Information Centre for School Facilities, Netherlands.[24]

Vast amounts are spent on building and equipping schools and colleges, so that they contain, in addition to classrooms, libraries and computer links, laboratories and technical workshops, auditoria, cafeterias, and sports and recreational facilities. Yet, school buildings, in particular, are often underutilised in time and as community and educational resources.

To maximise use of plant (but not increasing the amount of schooling students receive), a growing number of American school districts, jointly responsible for more than 2 000 schools, have introduced a year-round timetable. Typically, this involves students attending three of four terms a year, or in nine-week spells punctuated by three-week breaks. By staggering schedules, buildings can accommodate (and schools enrol) up to one-third more students. There are savings in spending on construction and, where students are bussed, school transport; and, while overall running costs obviously rise, per student costs usually decrease. On the debit side, in hot climates, air conditioning may need to be installed, and summer fuel bills can be high.

> In introducing a staggered schedule in one-third of its 700 schools, in 1990, the Los Angeles Unified School District had to spend $250 000 per elementary school and $640 000 per high school on installing air conditioning.

LOS ANGELES ◁

Introduced as a response to suburban growth, year-round schools are increasingly championed for their educational benefits, which include greater flexibility of enrolment, an enhanced curriculum (larger schools allowing greater specialisation), and improved student motivation and learning retention (due to the abolition of the long summer break).[25]

There is also growing public support in the United States for increasing the amount of schooling that students receive, which is another way of increasing the use of educational facilities. Since 1991, annual surveys have shown a majority in favour of 210 days a year compared with the now usual 180 days. Oregon passed legislation in 1992 to increase its year to 220 days in stages to 2010; Minnesota is adding two days a year to reach 190 by the autumn of 1994; and Kansas is extending its year to 186 days by 1995. However, proposals in four other states to add 20 days have been shelved because of cost. (In the 12-nation European Union the length of the school year ranges from 170 days in Spain to 207 days in some German *länder*, while in Japan it comprises 240 days.)

> Djanogly College, in Nottingham, England, has introduced a five-term year so that students attend 40 weeks a year (instead of the

NOTTINGHAM ◁

customary 38) – an annual gain of 10 days. Each term lasts eight weeks, spaced by two-week breaks (four in the summer). Additional benefits, according to the school's principal, include reducing the pressure on staff and students, by allowing more frequent rest periods and increasing the productivity of the school in the summer and autumn; in the traditional three-term system, school activity tends to wind down considerably in the run-up to the long summer break and takes a while to 'get back to speed' after it.[26] Although the pattern of breaks can present problems, parents and teachers have generally welcomed the new-style term, which has been organised so that seven of the 12 weeks of breaks coincide with those of other schools in the city.

The length of the school day and, more especially, the way in which students spend their time in school also varies widely. Comparing classtime in secondary schools in the European Union, Brian Knight found it ranged from just over 600 hours a year in some areas of Greece to double that throughout Italy.[27] In Japan, where children attend school on Saturday mornings, students receive as many as 1 500 hours of teaching a year.[28] (Knight found class hours a week varied between 17.25 and 30.)

The internal organisation of schools is a key factor in explaining differences, as it is also in making the most effective use of facilities. A British survey of primary schools found that the amount of time spent on registration and movement around the school varied between 1.7 hours and five hours a week, and on average it represented the equivalent of about 10 per cent of the 'taught week' – the time pupils are formally taught.[29]

▷ TELFORD

Secondary schools in some English cities are using plastic 'swipe cards' to cut registration time. Each student has a magnetic personal card which is used to 'self-register' attendance by passing the card through a reader. The reader records the 'swipe' and adds the student's name and the time to a database in the school's central computer. At Thomas Telford School, in Telford, there are two teacher-supervised 'swipes' in the classroom each day. (The cards are bar-coded so that they can also be used to make library loans. Other uses for the cards are as transport vouchers and in providing a 'cashless' cafeteria, whereby students are billed monthly for their purchases. Some schools have linked electronic noticeboards to the readers, enabling students to pick up messages as they 'swipe' their card. See the section on crime for more about swipe cards.)

The British survey found that four in five schools had increased their teaching hours since 1989. Most have achieved this within their existing day, but some have extended it – a development occurring in several countries which is linked to the introduction of new teaching methods and an enriched curriculum (see the case studies on city technology colleges and integrated lyceums).

Another way to make more use of educational facilities is to increase their clientele through community use, which may entail:

● new uses for existing facilities, such as rooms for meetings, cafeterias for social events, gymnasiums and sports fields for youth recreation and community sports programmes;

● creating facilities for community purposes, by incorporating them in the initial design, subsequent addition or remodelling spare capacity – for example, creating crèches, adapting a disused part of the building for small business offices or craft workshops, and integrating social services (housing offices, health centres); and

● community education, which may involve adults learning alongside students but is more likely to feature a separate programme of evening, weekend or vacation studies.

However, community use involves extra costs which may not fall to education budgets. There are, thus, questions of revenue and resourcing, as well as of management. Should the public pay as consumers or indirectly as taxpayers? Should charges be full cost or subsidised? Might payment be waived in return for voluntary work or other donations to schools? Do schools manage their own budgets, and have they the authority to operate commercially? Should school and non-school use be separately managed? Who pays for any initial development or building work?

There is another, less obvious sense in which facilities are underused, and that is in failing to realise the potential of premises in promoting learning. Buildings are often bleakly institutional, and grounds used only for physical education and play – a failing which is particularly regrettable in neighbourhoods that themselves are bleak and rundown. Creating urban gardens, ponds and farms, and setting up weather stations; decorating buildings through art projects; and creating environments which simulate facilities in the community (market squares, banks, law courts and offices, as in the so-called 'micro-society' schools) can have both curriculum and, as Michael Rutter and others have noted, behavioural benefits.

After studying differences between inner London secondary schools, Rutter found: "...schools varied greatly in how they responded to the physical conditions available to them. It was striking how very different essentially similar buildings could be made to appear. Some of the older buildings had been made pleasant and attractive places...; other schools, by contrast, had done little to transform their surroundings... variations in the care and decorations of buildings did prove to be related to [behavioural] outcome, although age [of buildings], considered alone, did not."[30]

In another British study[31], it was suggested that unwelcoming, drab and degraded school environments may have a brutalising effect on students. Conversely, well-managed and stimulating environments can help raise students' self-esteem. The study found that where schools had developed the building and grounds sensitively for play and teaching, positive changes in child behaviour had occurred.

Adult learners in colleges and schools

The impact of lifelong learning will force colleges to think of new ways of providing their services more flexibly. Learning opportunities will have to be personalised to the needs of individuals.
Michael Field, principal, Croydon College, London.[32]

Facility management beyond 2000 will be focused on the learning needs of students and clients rather than space and buildings.
John Bolton, principal, Blackburn College, England.[33]

More efficient means of contraception, legalised abortion, and the need for, and desire of, women to work make a new baby boom unlikely. Even with high immigration, and higher birth rates among minorities, developed countries will have fewer young people available to enter the workforce. At the same time, due to health care advances, earlier retirement, and the ageing of the 'baby boomers', the number of economically unproductive older people will grow considerably. As a result, the 'dependency ratio' will rise sharply: fewer will make the wealth, to generate the taxes, to support more.

Although unemployment is high now, it seems probable that, in the future, a greater proportion of the work-age population will need to be productive and, given the dearth of young recruits, 'new workers' have to be found from among the unemployed, 'women returners' and other hitherto marginalised groups, many of whom are undereducated or possess obsolete skills. In the words of the report endorsed by education ministers of the member countries of the OECD, in 1990: "OECD countries simply cannot afford to allow large pools of their potential talent to lie unexploited."[34]

Furthermore, the need for high and rising productivity among those in work will occur in a context of rapidly developing technologies and new materials, markets and work practices. This means a widening 'skills gap' faced by those re-entering the labour market; the prospect of increased dislocation in employment as more people can expect to change jobs and spend periods out of work; and the continuing need of those in work to update their knowledge and skills so as to maintain occupational competence. A committee of the Commission of the European Communities noted, also in 1990: "Though most of the technology that will be used in 10 years' time needs still to be developed, by 2000 at least 80 per cent of current employees will still be part of the labour force... a massive investment in upgrading of the existing workforce will be needed."[35]

These, rather than leisure purposes, are the forces driving the need for lifelong learning. In fact, there is no sharp distinction between vocationally-motivated and 'recreational' adult education. By raising self-esteem, education can give people the confidence to try and improve their work prospects or situation (including by going on to further study), while courses taken for 'personal interest', for example tuition in a foreign language, raise capability and may, eventually, bring benefits at work. An increasing number of companies recognise the connection between promoting education and the development of a learning culture conducive to flexibility and change at the workplace. Recent surveys by the Further Education Unit, carried out in London and Manchester, suggest that adult learning is best seen as a continuum in which the vocational element is more or less overt and job-specific: the majority saw participation in broad career, rather than narrow occupational, terms.[36]

Evening classes, full-time study, and on-the-job training will not be sufficient to cater for emerging demand. Colleges, in particular, must rethink their role and 'market', and how they are going to 'reach' it, including by taking the college to the community and making college premises and services more appropriate to the needs of adults.

● To make information and guidance more accessible, colleges are opening city-centre advice centres and creating 'outreach networks' using the premises of organisations in the community. (Both are necessary, as Her Majesty's Inspectors found, in Britain: "Guidance and information services... located in city centres... were virtually unknown to the residents of peripheral estates."[37])

> Handsworth College, in inner city Birmingham, targets minorities
> (who make up 53 per cent of the district's residents) and the
> unemployed through a city centre 'drop-in' advice and learning centre.
> It also runs activities at city libraries, jobcentres (employment offices),
> the premises of government-subsidised temporary employment
> schemes, and at places of worship – notably, pentecostal churches,
> mosques and gurdwaras.[38]

BIRMINGHAM ◁

> Another college in England runs a series of programmes called 'New
> Directions' about five times a year. Each is located in a primary

school or church hall in a different part of its catchment area and is publicised via the school or community group which sponsored it. The programmes, which are free of charge, enable participants to review their present position, to learn about the availability of education, training and work in the locality and to make personal development plans.

● 'Remote' learning centres are being set up, either as college-run premises, in rented accommodation, or in collaboration with community organisations and schools; and buses and trailers are being converted as mobile education and advice units. These help overcome barriers to participation caused by lack of car ownership and inadequate public transport. However, community-based provision in some areas may not succeed unless accompanied by a local crime prevention scheme.

▷ BIRMINGHAM

By introducing a 'quality system', East Birmingham College, in England, was able to eliminate one entire level of management, and spent the savings on redesigning the college and extending its work through the development of 15 inner-city sites. The idea is to help foster community contacts through a strong local identity. The college has specified that 20 per cent of every programme area be offered in the inner city.[39]

▷ LONDON

The Mobile Employment and Training Advice Project in the Finsbury Park district of London uses a converted public transport bus to target three inner city housing projects. On board are professional advisers, mobile phones, reference material, a video training facility and micro-computers. Half of those who use the bus go on to further studies or get jobs. A report in Britain concluded: "Mobile units provide an excellent response to the need for sharing scarce resources... the flexibility of time, duration and place makes mobile delivery attractive to many customers."[40]

● On campus, centres are being established which are 'open access' (not requiring customary entry criteria), 'drop-in' (as opposed to by appointment, or timetabled use), and 'flexible' (featuring courses individualised in terms of content, time and place). There are also an increasing number of conference, seminar and residential facilities which have been specially created to cater for the corporate updating and training market.

Developments such as these are being supported by the creation of crèches and childcare facilities; the use of telecommunications in networking, including home links and computer loan schemes; revised catering arrangements; streamlined adult registration procedures often linked to the remodelling of foyers and reception areas; and refurbished social areas.[41]

Image in the community is important as a statement of colleges' new mission, and this extends to the condition and layout of buildings. As the report on British upper secondary schools and colleges, already quoted, reminds: "16-plus year-olds are under no compulsion to attend; they can go away if they do not like what they see. So how the college welcomes newcomers and receives its students is important for its success."[42]

Accompanying the increase in adult learners is the trend in education from timetabled teaching to student-centred learning. Less time is spent in timetabled spaces and more in resource centres (formerly libraries) or in working alone or in small groups. Rigid subject departmental structures are giving to way to the organisation of colleges' work in programme areas. And, greater importance is being accorded to learner support services.

In future, a facilities strategy will have to consider: flexibility versus efficiency; on-campus as against remote facilities, outreach activities and work- and home-based study; whether to own, lease or rent accommodation; sole management as opposed to partnership arrangements, networking and multi-agency approaches; the balance between general, centralised facilities and those that are specialised or customised for particular groups; and the use of computers and telecommunications, internally and externally, in learning and management.

Schools, too, may provide a venue for adult learning, although many potential participants will resist a return to a place associated with past failure. Successful uses include community-based recreational evening classes and remedial basic education where parents learn alongside their children.

The place of vocational education and training

...what I want is to give Tom a good eddication; an eddication as'll be a bread to him.
Mr Tulliver, father, in *The Mill on The Floss*, by George Eliot.[43]

The prize will go to those countries that are organized as national learning systems, and where all institutions are organized to learn and to act on what they learn.
Ray Marshall and Marc Tucker, *Thinking for a Living*.[44]

Where we work, how we work, and what sort of work we do – even whether we work at all – are aspects of our lives that have changed considerably in the last quarter century.

- Manufacturing output has increased, but automation means far fewer operatives are needed: the market for unskilled or narrowly-skilled workers is fast disappearing, while new work practices emphasise multi-skilling and team-working. There is, thus, the need for a broader-based training – incorporating the concept of core skills – as well as higher levels of skills.

● The number of professional and managerial jobs is growing, but entry requires university-level qualifications.

● Service sector and retail jobs have greatly increased; although many are 'minimum wage' and part-time, they require a raised level of basic education.

● Self-employment is also growing, as is competition and the need for continual innovation in methods and product lines: more people need business skills and knowledge of entrepreneurship.

● Most women work, and they rightly aspire to the same opportunities as men; this has implications for gender-bias in vocational education and training.

● There is the paradox of a growing workforce and high rates of unemployment; this poses a challenge to the flexibility of training arrangements and their responsiveness to change in industry, commerce and the public sector.

Cities have felt the impact of some of these trends particularly hard. Inner city factories have moved to new sites and regions where highways are more accessible and land costs cheaper. Chicago lost one-third of its industrial jobs in the 1980s. Marseille has lost a quarter of its since the mid-1980s. New service jobs are often in the suburbs and inaccessible to those dependent on public transport, while high-profile downtown retail developments, such as Baltimore's Inner Harbor, do not compensate for the loss of relatively well-paid manufacturing jobs.

Unemployment, which on average has accounted for about one in ten of the workforce in most OECD countries since the early-1980s, is often substantially higher in inner cities, where it particularly affects the under-25s and racial and ethnic minorities. British urbanologist Robin Hambleton estimates that minorities are twice as likely as whites to be out of work[45], and in the view of Christopher Jencks at no time since 1975 have fewer than one in five 'non-white' American men in their early-20s been idle – neither in work, including in the armed services, nor in education.[46]

In the wake of these developments, vocational education and training is struggling to chart a new direction – one that answers afresh the basic questions 'What preparation do young people require to establish themselves in employment?' and 'What knowledge and skills can employers expect of new recruits?' Answers to both imply potentially far-reaching consequences for the planning and use of facilities.

Early specialisation is falling out of favour. Instead, the move is towards a broad and more balanced curriculum centred on a foundation of knowledge and skills deemed necessary for employment as well as further study. Raised standards and increased content suggest that basic education should extend to the end of compulsory schooling. Within this 'common core' the vocational and technical element needs modernising and strengthening to reflect changes in the labour market and work practices.

● Craft-based (and often gender-biased) options, such as woodwork, metalwork and home economics, are being replaced by 'technology studies' taken by all students (see the case studies on city technology colleges and integrated lyceums). New specialist accommodation is needed, involving the addition of new facilities and the regrouping and re-equipping of rooms.

UNITED KINGDOM ◁

Since 1991 the UK government has run a scheme – the Technology Schools Initiative – to promote good technology teaching and vocational developments for 14-16 year-olds. Schools submit bids for project money – about $37 million a year – which are evaluated by a team of experts. Technical advice seminars are run in different cities, to help schools draw up their proposals, which must link curriculum development with accommodation improvement plans. About 100 schools a year receive grants.

A school catering for 900 boys aged 11-18, in a former textile town with high unemployment and a large ethnic minority population (contributing 40 per cent of pupils), received a grant for $375 000 in 1992. Although built in 1960, much of the school's technical equipment was already second-hand. Apart from minor refurbishments by teachers and some decoration in 1980, no modernisation or improvement had taken place. With its grant, nine rooms used for technology were refurbished to create high-quality provision for biotechnology, construction, control technology, computer-aided design and manufacture, electronics, engineering and food technology. The project was carried out by a private company and managed by the school's head of technology. Subsequently, the school's technology environment has been upgraded from 'poor' to 'very good'; inspectors commented: "...substantial changes were achieved in a very short time, helped by a clear policy for development, hard work on the part of the teachers and the good quality of management within technology."[47]

● Pre-vocational studies programmes are being introduced, involving 'taster' courses, work experience, and 'enterprise studies' designed to enhance students' appreciation of business and employment. Some schools are creating simulated work environments, while others have adopted vocationally-related themes that require specialised laboratory or workshop spaces.

▷   L O N D O N   The Walworth World of Work is a simulated office environment occupying the top floor of Walworth School in south London. With funds from companies and development agencies, and jointly planned by teachers and company personnel, it is used by 15 and 16 year-olds to work on 'mini-enterprise' projects.

▷   L O W E L L   The adoption, in the early-1980s, of a 'micro-society' curriculum by City Magnet School, in Lowell, Massachusetts, led to a complete renovation of facilities. Students (aged 10-13) learn about the principles of publishing, economics and government, and put their skills into practice at 'jobs' carried out in simulated environments within the school, including a mock newspaper office, bank, marketplace and courtroom.

● Information technology is being implemented throughout the primary and secondary curriculum, and study and career guidance is being given more prominence. School-wide IT networks and external 'high-tech' links are required, as is a greater variety of spaces, including for large and small group work, individual study, counselling, and use by 'outside' experts and personnel who are supporting the school's work – including through school-business partnerships.

Post-16, the expectation is now firmly that young people should continue in some form of studies and/or training until at least the age of 18. In the United States, this is the age of high school graduation; in Germany, there is a legal requirement for at least part-time participation; while in Sweden, failure to complete upper secondary school is tantamount to declaring oneself 'unemployable'.

However, except where post-compulsory participation has been historically low, as in the United Kingdom, or population shifts defy birth trends (in the American south and west), increased staying on is not resulting in greater absolute numbers. The changes that are occurring in vocational education and training – and many countries have reformed their arrangements in the last decade – are essentially qualitative, involving a rationalisation of provision, facilities and qualifications.[48]

The broad direction of these reforms is toward a unified and more coherent system, with easier movement and parity of esteem between vocational and academic elements as well as between vocational streams and higher education. Also, the reforms aim to make education and training more responsive to changing labour market needs, by placing emphasis on core skills and progressive specialisation and increasing the involvement of employers and local communities in planning.

Thus, the 1991 reforms in Denmark saw the combination of basic vocational training with apprenticeship and technician courses into a new system centred on broadly-based qualifications within individual specialisations. In Germany, the number of 'recognised occupations' within the apprenticeship system has been reduced through amalgamation, leading to more common training arrangements. In France, the number of specialisms within initial vocational education is being reduced. While, in the United Kingdom, the new National Vocational Qualifications framework is resulting in the creation of new and revised qualifications within a coherent national system.

Several questions arise 'post-16':

● Is there still a place for colleges (or schools) which teach a narrow vocational curriculum, or should they be amalgamated with others to provide a broader subject base, possibly allowing for the study of both vocational and academic courses? Countries with 'weak' apprenticeship systems, such as Britain and France, are putting emphasis on flexible progression routes. On the other hand, German employers have resisted co-ordination between full-time vocational education (in *berufsfachschulen*) and the part-time, day-release *berufsschule* system. In Hamburg, a city of 1.6 million people, approximately 50 000 part-time students attend as many as 48 monotechnic *berufsschulen*.

● How do arrangements for initial vocational education and training connect with those for unemployed young people taking part in government-subsidised training schemes and adults learners wanting to update their skills or retrain?

● At what stage does access to workshop facilities become essential, and where should these be located – in colleges (or schools), in publicly-funded industrial and business training centres, in centres set up by groups of firms within an industry or sector, or on the premises of individual firms and organisations? What is the most effective and efficient solution in terms of public investment?

CERTA is a technology resource centre located near the headquarters of Renault, at Billancourt in the suburbs of Paris. Funded by the car firm and national and regional government, it provides access to advanced technology equipment not available in schools.[49]

PARIS ◁

Techtrain is a community technology and enterprise centre in Salford, an inner city borough in Greater Manchester. Built on a secondary school campus, the centre was jointly funded by Salford City Council, local colleges, community organisations and companies. It provides state-of-the art equipment in engineering, electronics and science for use by schools and colleges, as well as firms, associations and individuals.

SALFORD ◁

▷ BERLIN

Apprentices at Mercedes-Benz, in Berlin, receive all their technical training and basic vocational education in-house (normally, German apprentices attend college on day-release for the equivalent of two days a week). The company runs both an education centre and a workshop and office training complex. These enable close training and staff development links with actual production, and information on new product developments, including those not yet available on the market, can be built into basic technical training.

Uncoupling schools and buildings

When resources are limited, it is important to look at the capacity of other buildings to meet learning requirements, and not maintain the narrow view that education must occur within the four walls of a schoolhouse.
Business Roundtable, *Participation Guide: A Primer for Business on Education.*[50]

...an entrepreneurial society challenges habits and assumptions of schooling and learning... the basic architectural plan on which our schools and universities are built goes back three hundred years and more.
Peter F. Drucker, *Innovation and Entrepreneurship.*[51]

We build schools and we attend them: so close has the association been between the institution and the buildings it occupies that 'school' is used, with equal facility, for both. Yet, as we have seen, the linkage is being eroded in several ways.

● Schools and colleges buy 'non-educational' facilities for specialised or short-term use, such as buses as mobile education units and houses for temporary conversion to classrooms.

● They rent space in commercial buildings, including in 'strategic' locations such as shopping areas.

▷ MINNEAPOLIS

In the 4.5 million sq. ft. Mall of America outside Minneapolis/St Paul, five school districts have collaborated to set up a 'learning laboratory' which incorporates pre-school childcare, after-school activities, an early-grade elementary school, provision for adult learning, a centre where high school students can combine studies and work experience gained through part-time jobs in the shopping mall, and an 'exploratorium' – a facility for educational visits.

● Tuition and educational services are delivered remotely, using technology links, by means of outreach activities, or through consortium, partnership or franchising arrangements. Often, these involve the use of premises owned and run by other organisations.

● School and college buildings are used for educational and non-education purposes by individuals and groups in the community; conversely, schools are housed in multi-use community facilities.

Several factors are at work in relaxing the traditional association between schools as institutions and dedicated (public) buildings. There is the need for a greater diversity of types of space, partly to improve access for learners and 'customers'; new possibilities are being opened up by technologies; and there is the planning and management emphasis on flexibility, efficiency and reduced costs.

In Tilburg, in the Netherlands, schools are experimenting with revised schedules which allow students to use computer links to study at home. Arrangements have been made so that every student has the necessary equipment to be able to take part, using computers to work interactively with teachers from home one or two days a week.

TILBURG

Similar schemes involving the use of low-cost word processors are being piloted in Britain. At a primary school in Camden, an inner London borough, 11 year-olds are each issued with a portable computer for use in school and at home. Home-based assignments are set, and parents contract with the school to record their child's progress in a diary as well as to take reasonable care of the equipment in respect of damage and security.

LONDON

In Golden Grove, a suburb of Adelaide, a secular and a parochial school share a campus which includes a common auditorium, gymnasium and sports facilities, and a refectory. These shared facilities are jointly managed and their use maximised through staggered timetabling.[52]

ADELAIDE

In planning expanded provision for 16-18 year-olds, Thomas Telford School (mentioned above) has decided not to increase its physical capacity along 'normal' lines, but to build an open learning centre, with the aim of delivering 30 per cent of its courses for the age-group via distance learning by 1996. The school also intends to connect to a regional cable network, to broadcast courses direct to students in their homes, thereby expanding its 'market' to adult learners.

TELFORD

Another factor is the growth in off-campus components in the curriculum. Over 90 per cent of British 14-16 year-olds now take part in work experience, which, for the majority, is assessed towards the school leaving qualification. In Atlanta, high school students must carry out 75 hours of voluntary service at one of several hundred approved centres, and a similar graduation requirement has recently been introduced in the State of Maryland.

Accompanying this development is the move from curricula that lay down, often rigid, times to be spent on particular subjects towards competence-based schemes which are more flexible and shift the focus from attendance to learning. "As soon as you say that performance is the key," says Theodore R. Sizer, chairman of the Coalition of Essential Schools, one of the United States' leading education reform groups, "then things like mandatory attendance and always being in a school building are going to become less and less important."[53]

Some education authorities have seized on this logic to innovate; they have accepted that the standard model of schooling need not, indeed should not, be applied to all.

● Alternative programmes and schools are being set up, offering flexible scheduling and 'unschool-like' learning environments.

▷ SAN DIEGO

Instead of dropping out, students in San Diego can attend a learning centre which provides an alternative route to graduation. Housed in two portable buildings at a high school, the centre is open from 7 am to 9.30 pm daily and year-round. It is designed to look like an office, rather than a classroom, with an informal layout of conference tables and computer stations, and provides childcare for student parents. Students attend in groups of 20 for two hours a day, half of which is spent working at computers on individual assignments. In addition, they each have an hour-long meeting with a teacher and carry out about 15 hours of independent study each week. The curriculum is the same as for other students, but work can be paced to fit in with full- or part-time jobs. About 2 000 students a year attend, and 60 per cent go on to college. The school district's dropout rate has been halved.

▷ DENMARK

In Denmark, more than 80 'production schools' for 16-19 year-olds have been set up to cater for high school dropouts. Usually located on publicly-owned former industrial premises, but sometimes on farms or in school buildings, the schools eschew a combination of classroom tuition and workplace training in favour of integrating teaching with actual production in metallurgy and other crafts. The schools are set up by local government but run by an independent manager and are governed by an elected board partly drawn from employer organisations and labour unions.

Standardised arrangements are also being modified under pressure for greater diversity among schools; some are being broken up into smaller units designed to provide a stable and personalised 'family' environment for students, particularly in urban areas with a high incidence of social problems.

● Schools are being organised differently, including the creation of 'schools within schools'; and new types of public school are being established which do not require traditional, or purpose-built, facilities.

Köln-Kolweide is a secondary school with 2 000 students, in Cologne, which uses team teaching, co-operative learning and peer tutoring. On entering the school, aged 11, students are placed in groups of 85 to 90 which remain together with the same team of six to eight teachers for six years. Classrooms have no 'front' or rows of desks. Instead, students sit around tables, working with the same 'table group' of five or six students (integrated by sex, ability and ethnic origin) for at least a year. The table group is the basic unit of learning. "If a student has a problem," explains the principal, Anne Ratzki, "he doesn't have to wait for a teacher; he can ask his table group for help. If the group can't help, then the teacher will – but the first responsibility lies with the group."[54]

COLOGNE

In New York, about 50 'New Visions' schools are being planned, most to cater for between 500 and 700 high school students. The initiative, which began in 1992, is based on the success of reformed schools in one of the city's poorest districts, East Harlem. In the mid-1970s, student test scores ranked bottom of those for the 32 districts, but a decade later they had reached par with those for the rest of New York. The reform involved the replacement of the existing schools with small, thematic, alternative schools, which students and parents choose rather than are assigned.

NEW YORK

"We believed that a school is not just a building," says Seymour Fliegel, who developed the programme, "and so we often grouped several small, alternative schools within the walls of a single traditional public-school building... It was further decided that no one would be forced into a failing school; those that could not attract or keep students would be shut down. Because schools were small, taking up only a portion of a public school building, shutting one down only meant abandoning a failed idea, not demolishing bricks and mortar. A new school could be tried in its place..."[55]

In Minnesota, the uncoupling of institutions and buildings has been taken a step further: since 1991, groups of teachers have been able to start and run independent public schools – 'charter schools' – under contract with school districts. These are legally incorporated and free from most state and local regulations. Contracts set performance standards for renewal, and funding 'follows' students on a per capita

ST PAUL

basis according to enrolment (which can be any size). Charter schools do not have distinct buildings: any number could coexist in the same building, or a school may occupy several, quite different buildings.

City Academy in St Paul is housed in a community centre where there is also a daycare programme. It has 30 students, exclusively consisting of 'hard core' dropouts, who have attempted (and failed) to continue attendance at publicly-funded, but city-run, alternative schools. The academy provides teaching from 8 am to 1.30 pm three days a week. On the remaining two days, there are 'enrichment' activities (music, art, work with computers) and 'community-based experience' (helping to rehabilitate housing, taking part in craft workshops, working in local museums). Class sizes are very small, and students set their own rules for conduct and discipline. The school hires (and fires) its teachers, and makes its own premises and equipment arrangements.

Most buildings will continue to be used as they have been, as dedicated environments for single institutions. Nevertheless, established notions of time and space in education will be increasingly challenged due to the emphasis on learning outcomes, curricula which look beyond the classroom, and greater diversity among schools, including in the way they are organised and governed.

III

Living in the City

Joseph Fernandez, the former superintendent of Miami and New York schools, says there can be no "putting the smoke back into [the] cigar": the social context in which schools carry out their work has changed irredeemably in the last 30 years. He cites research by the California Department of Education which showed that in the 1980s the 'top ten' student offences committed on school property were headed by drug abuse, and included rape, robbery, assault and arson (with absenteeism and extortion not far behind).[56]

The extent to which social issues have been taken on by urban schools in the United States is shown in the first annual baseline indicators report of The Council of the Great City Schools, published in September 1992. This found that, in 1990-91, a wider range of socially-related services and education programmes were provided in some, and often all, schools in the 47 largest urban districts, which the council represents. Included were childcare for the infants of teenage mothers; parenting for teenagers and adults; 'latch key' and after-school schemes; drugs education; AIDS and sexually-transmitted disease prevention; support for the children of drug-addicted parents; suicide and stress reduction for students; crime and gang prevention; pregnancy prevention; and assistance for homeless children.[57]

While some education authorities resist an expanded role for schools in dealing with the social context of learning, pointing out that it is not for schools to solve social problems, others argue that an holistic approach is essential if overall levels of educational achievement are to be raised. The next section looks at some of the issues and illustrates what can be done.

Families and Poverty

...the education crisis that is going to kill us... is the large number of bright kids who fall out of the mainstream because their families are not functioning.
James P. Comer, psychiatrist, Yale University Child Study Center.[58]

...schools and social service providers must be closely linked. Social service agencies are like suppliers to a company and are essential to the quality of a student's education.

National Alliance of Business, *A Blueprint for Business on Restructuring Education.*[59]

Children today are much more likely than a generation ago to experience family disruption, and to grow up in poor households and without the benefit of a regular male presence as a result. In nearly all developed countries at least one family in ten with dependent children is headed by a single parent. Often it is substantially more: one in seven in Britain and Sweden, and more than one in four in the United States. Among some minority groups it is still higher (as many as 57 per cent of African-American families are single-parent).

Single parenthood is often accompanied by poverty. A report by the US Census Bureau shows that the income of households with children whose parents have separated declines, on average, by 37 per cent within four months of the break up, almost doubling the proportion of children living below the federal poverty line.[60] By this definition, half the single mothers in the USA are poor (compared to one in ten married couples). International research shows that children in single-parent families in Australia, Canada, Germany and the United Kingdom are about four times more likely than under-18s generally to be living in poverty.[61]

In addition to poverty, the rise of single parenthood has been accompanied by, or resulted in, a number of other developments, with consequences for education.

More children are bereft of any contact with their fathers. The National Survey of Children in the United States found that almost half of the children in single-parent families did not see their father at all in the previous year, and only one in six saw them weekly. Even where contact is regularly maintained, the role of fathers changes. As Barbara Dafoe Whitehead describes it: "Instead of providing steady advice and guidance, divorced fathers become 'treat' dads."[62] Also, there is an increased risk of children not having any parent. One in 15 African-American and one in 25 Latino children in the United States now live in households without either parent present – the so called zero-parent family.

The increased proportion of women in the workforce, allied to the limitations of single-parent domestic arrangements, means that many more children spend long hours fending for themselves. A survey of American 14 year-olds indicates that about 27 per cent spend two or more hours at home alone after school each day. In poor households the time tends to be longer (one school-age child in five is alone for more than three hours), and in poor districts the numbers involved are greater. One response is the growth of after-school (or latch key) programmes.

Children in single-parent families are two to three times as likely as those in two-parent families to have emotional and behavioural problems. At school, a disproportionate number behave aggressively and pose disciplinary problems, and they are much more disposed to drop out. They are also more likely to fall foul of the law (in the USA, more than 70 per cent of all juveniles in state reform institutions come from fatherless homes).

Finally, there is the link between poverty, poor housing and educational success. Overcrowded homes and dangerous and decaying neighbourhoods, lacking play areas and other facilities, are obvious potential handicaps. But many children of poor families are frequently 'on the move', living in hostels and switching schools, if they attend at all. In the USA, it is estimated that school-age children comprise a quarter of the homeless. Comments Joyce Epstein of Johns Hopkins University: "Educators have grown up a lot about not assuming everyone has two parents. But they often slip [when talking] about 'your room', 'where you do your homework' and some of the accouterments people have or things they own."[63]

A number of implications for, and possible interventions by, education can be identified. These include mentoring programmes; sex and health education which recognises earlier sexual maturity among teenagers and the existence of AIDS; counselling and therapeutic components in the curriculum, including, importantly, those designed to raise student self-esteem; the possibility of providing residential accommodation in some schools; and ways of reducing the disruption of education for those in families frequently 'on the move', including the homeless.

In addition, reference earlier in this essay was made to school 'return to learn' and remedial education classes which allow adults to gain qualifications to enhance their job prospects; the use of school cafeterias and integrated welfare and nutrition education programmes to assist in ensuring that children of low-income households are adequately and properly fed; and the possibility of education authorities and individual schools employing older students and parents in minor repair, cleaning, and night cafeteria work to supplement family income.

However, education is not social services, and planners should be wary of 'the marginal' encroaching on what is essential. Ultimately, schools are judged, by their students as by the wider community they serve, on their success in teaching and learning. There is also the risk of social engineering, when the approach ought to be practical and realistic. For example, three broad areas where action can be taken which assists families are through the provision of good quality childcare and 'early learning', and of activities and facilities that enable school-age young people to be cared for and supervised outside normal school hours, and the combination of social, health and other services in integrated family support centres located on, or near, school premises.

Childcare and nursery schools

Publicly-funded daycare not only enables more women to work, it also raises the quality of care received by children who might, otherwise, be left with neighbours, child-minders or poorly-resourced private care centres. In addition, nursery education – from the age of three – "leads to immediate and lasting social and educational benefits".[64]

The lack of quality care and a universal entitlement to nursery education especially affects those in poor districts, where there is often a higher than average proportion of homes headed by lone mothers and families are less likely to be able to afford books and toys. Where provision is insufficient, it is the poor who suffer from the competition for places.[65]

▷ BIRMINGHAM

Describing the situation in Handsworth, Birmingham, in 1985, Dervla Murphy notes that 43 per cent of the children registered at nursery schools (for three and four year-olds) were from single-parent families. Yet, there was only one place for every three children, while government-funded day nurseries (for younger children) each had waiting lists of up to 150 children. As a result, many children spend most of their first five years in daycare, says Murphy, who adds: "I was reliably informed [by mothers] that the average child-minder provides very restricted play-space, few toys, no books, poor food and little if any individual attention... and the children's restlessness and noisiness is often curbed by methods that can do permanent psychological damage."[66]

School inspectors in England – where only two in five three year-olds take part in publicly-funded pre-schooling – found a marked variance in the extent and quality of provision between cities as well as within them.[67] Co-ordination between local government and voluntary agencies was poor, funding inconsistent, and continuity of provision threatened by the heavy reliance on the use of volunteers; parents in poor districts were least informed about existing opportunities, and least equipped to find out.

Research in several countries shows that pre-schooling most benefits the disadvantaged, and not only educationally but in terms of improved socialisation. In the United States, disadvantaged youngsters with good pre-school education are almost twice as likely as those without it to be in work and able to support themselves when they reach adulthood; the presence of pre-schooling has also been positively correlated to increased high school graduation and reduced involvement in crime.[68]

Arguments in favour of pre-schooling as a social investment (quite apart from considerations of gender equality) are gaining ground, so that more countries are likely to seek to emulate the situation in Belgium and France, where all children have the right to be accepted in free nursery schools (*écoles maternelles*), or infant schools attached to primary schools, from the age of two and a half years and three years, respectively.

New Zealand has set a target of 95 per cent of three and four year-olds in nursery education by 2001. It has created a new early childhood sector which integrates education and care, with equal status with other sectors of education and its own funding system. A national Early Childhood Development Unit has been set up, to provide co-ordination, training and support – with graded increases in funding over a four-year period. The present diversity of services is to be maintained, but funding will depend on the achievement of nationally-set standards.

NEW ZEALAND ◁

Research also underlines that the key to benefits is quality – in terms of teachers and carers, staffing ratios, facilities, and the style of learning, which should aim at confidence-building and the acquisition of learning techniques, not simply that of knowledge. Good practice includes:

● Environments which are well-planned, stimulating, secure and healthy; provide a variety of learning experiences indoors and out, space for movement and small, intimate areas for rest and quiet; and promote 'purposeful play'.

● Good home-school links – including the use of school liaison teachers to visit children's homes to aid the transition to education; parental assistance in class; parents' lounges in schools (regarded as especially important to effect social contact and mutual support among mothers in areas of public housing); and schemes that help improve the learning environment at home, such as the use of toy libraries.

Out-of-hours schemes[69]

In Murfreesboro, a city near Nashville, Tennessee, children may spend as many as 12 hours in school as part of the school district's extended day programme. Parents may drop off children as early as 6 am at each of the city's elementary schools. After play and physical exercises in the gymnasium, breakfast is provided before classes start at 7.45 am. After-school activities include homework tutorials, sports and recreational activities, extra classes in science, art or a foreign language, and private music lessons.

MURFREESBORO ◁

Parents foot the bill for most of the costs of the extended day – about $26 per child per week during the schoolyear and $40 per week in the summer vacation, when schools retain the same opening hours. Costs are kept low by the use of student teachers from the local university and regular teachers who want to work part-time or put in extra hours at a lower than normal rate.

Many schools and school districts are not as enthusiastic providers as Murfreesboro's, however. A survey sponsored by the British government, in 1990, found that only four per cent of schools (in England) ran an out-of-school scheme, with a further one per cent about to do so and 11 per cent considering it; the vast majority had no plans. Most of the schemes were in the inner boroughs of London, where playcentres operate most evenings and, in some cases, during vacations at nearly half of the schools.

The report of the survey, published by the Kids' Clubs Network, found that: "Schools raised a large number of issues and problems relating to the location of out-of-school schemes in school buildings. The largest number related to lack of a suitable room to hold the scheme in. There was a general feeling that an out-of-school scheme could not be held in a classroom, both because of concern about damage to displays and equipment, and because it was felt that children needed a change of scenery in which to relax after the day's school." Some schools said it would be difficult to organise a scheme because buildings were cleaned at that time.[70]

Another restraint was funding, especially since the introduction of school-based management, as rules for delegated budgets specify that money must be spent on education, which excludes play and care schemes. Three-quarters of the schools surveyed said they would have to obtain alternative sources of funding if they were to run a scheme, and most felt that charging fees would deter participation.

A study by the US Education Department, presented to Congress in the winter of 1993, showed that virtually no school schemes had access to the entire building; most share space with other children and staff; and one in four did not have access to a playground or park. School-based schemes were also less likely to operate in summer, during holidays, and after 6 pm. The department's recommendations included greater commitment from school principals in "insuring adequate space within facilities"; giving children more freedom to rearrange space for activities; and providing interest areas that are "inviting and homelike".[71]

In the United States, about a quarter of schemes are based in public schools. The remainder are run by companies, non-profit and religious organisations, colleges and universities, and parent and community groups, as well as by branches of local government other than the school board. One way school districts could promote after-school provision is by working with some of these organisations as partners. By contributing technical expertise, making available public buildings (not necessarily schools) and equipment, and, perhaps, subsidising staff costs, many financially hard-pressed but successful neighbourhood initiatives, particularly in poor districts, could improve the quality of their provision and surroundings.

Family resource centres

Integrated approaches to service provision are springing up in several parts of the United States.

The South Bronx is a predominantly African-American and Latino district, immediately north of Manhattan, which is characterised by severe social deprivation and physical blight. It has been chosen as the location for four 'educare centers', being built in a first-time collaboration between New York's board of education and the city's housing authority. The intention is to create facilities which have an early childhood and community focus as part of schemes to rehabilitate adjacent public housing for those on low incomes, including the homeless.

NEW YORK ◁

The four-storey buildings include educational facilities for kindergarten, grade one and grade two children (ages 6-8); daycare and play areas for younger children; after-school recreational facilities for up to 10 year-olds; and provision for parent and community programmes, including parent rooms and offices for medical and social workers.

As a joint approach, by the two agencies, the scheme is expected to be more cost-effective (the housing authority usually builds separate community facilities) and to enable more mothers to work or to continue studies, while also achieving educational benefits through improved parenting.

In Florida, legislation passed in 1991 allocates grants for competitive bidding by school districts to create 'full service schools', which "integrate education, medical and/or social and human services that are beneficial to meeting the needs of children and youth and their families on school grounds or in locations which are easily accessible".

FLORIDA ◁

The state argues that schools are appropriate locations for providing a wide range of services. People are more likely to know the location of schools than they are the whereabouts of agency offices. School buildings often have surplus space that could be assigned to agencies without incurring extra public expenditure. Students attending health or other appointments can return directly to class afterwards rather than miss half a day, or more, of schooling. And, agency workers can collaborate more easily with teachers on particular cases, as well as on programmes aimed at prevention. In addition, a 'one stop shop' fosters communication between agencies, can reduce duplication, and saves parents' time.

▷ SAN DIEGO

The New Beginnings programme in San Diego was started in 1988, it involves city and county government, the city's school board and housing authority, a children's hospital, a university medical centre, and a community college in a collaboration covering family and health services and adult education. The programme is funded through normal budgets, rather than 'soft' project money, and those taking part have to adopt a shared statement of philosophy committing them to the scheme.

The first New Beginnings centre was built in new premises adjacent to Hamilton Elementary School, in east San Diego, a district with the city's highest housing density and crime rate, the second highest rate of child abuse, and one of the lowest average household incomes in the county. When the collaborating agencies pooled their information they found that the city's social services department alone was providing $5.3 million a year in services to students at the school and their families, at an administrative cost of $500 000.

The centre is used for school registration so that families can become familiar with its services and it is staffed by 'family service advocates', drawn from agency personnel, who provide information about services, counselling, and develop plans to help families move towards self-sufficiency. Health examinations and immunizations are provided, as well as mental health services, a supplementary nutrition programme, and adult education classes including in English as a second language. An extended team of agency professionals, not based at the centre, is involved in casework, and encompasses, among others, the police and probation services, the parks and recreation department, library services, and the public housing authority.

Race and Ethnicity

Even when we are here for years, I know I wouldn't feel that I am European. Maybe our children will.
Ahmed Jasim, Iraqi Kurd, Hallefors refugee camp, Sweden.[72]

The first shock to an African child entering school is that his world is not worth learning about.
Chenjerai Hove, Zimbabwean broadcaster.[73]

Education systems in urban areas in developed countries increasingly serve a multicultural and ethnically diverse population. The education of minorities is a complex subject which goes beyond the scope of this report, nonetheless it is reasonable to ask whether there are ways in which school and college facilities could be better used to serve the needs of minorities. But, before that, a few observations are in order.

Firstly, the evidence from many countries shows that, in general, children in racial and ethnic minorities tend to underachieve at school. In the four largest cities in the Netherlands (Amsterdam, The Hague, Rotterdam and Utrecht), minority students are much more likely than 'indigenous Dutch' 13-18 year-olds to be in the two lowest status and least academic of the four available streams.[74] Similarly, in Germany fewer than four per cent of Turks achieve places in academic secondary schools (*gymnasien*) compared with about 30 per cent of Germans. In the United Kingdom, the Swann Committee concluded, in 1985, that "West Indian children are not doing at all well in the educational system",[75] and a House of Commons report in the same year found that half of the Chinese students in London and two-thirds in Manchester left school without a qualification in English.[76]

The overall underachievement of Latino and African-American students in the United States is well documented, and persists despite substantial improvement in education standards, generally, in the last 20 years. As Claude M. Steele has pointed out, school is often a negative experience for African-Americans: "Despite socio-economic disadvantages as a group, blacks begin school with test scores that are fairly close to test scores of whites their age. The longer they stay in school, however, the more they fall behind. By the time of sixth grade, blacks in many school districts are two full grades behind whites in achievement."[77]

Secondly, the ethnic composition of schools varies widely, even within the same school district, and it changes over time, and these differences should be reflected in the practical arrangements of schools. Where, say, a quarter of a school's students are Vietnamese, that is the salient fact, not that the school has become in some imprecise way 'multicultural'. Equally, the particular needs of different religions represented among a school population may need to be taken into account.

Nevertheless, schools prepare students for life in society at large, so an approach which emphasises pluralism is also required. Crucially, no minority group should feel excluded from the educational process, and this involves a reappraisal of the position of the majority and not only steps to accommodate minorities. As a black American academic, Molefi Kete Asante, has put it: "[It] is not an idea to replace all things European, but to expand the dialogue... to locate African-American children in the center of the information being presented in classrooms across the nation..."[78]

Thirdly, the situation often experienced by African-American children – and, increasingly, by some ethnic groups in Europe – is one where the minority forms the majority in a school, but the school remains shaped by the ethos and rules of an educational system in which they comprise a minority.

In most urban school districts in the USA, African-Americans are by far the dominant group, a situation largely brought about because white parents have chosen to withdraw their children to private schools, or move to 'whiter' suburbs, rather than see them 'integrated'. In the 47 largest urban school districts in the United States, overall, only one student in four is white.

▷   DETROIT   Cities such as Detroit have found that integration has left them with the worst of all worlds. When, in 1975, it sought to integrate schools across school district boundaries, which would, in effect, have brought the city's 250 000 children into a common system with some 500 000 children in 53 suburban districts, the US Supreme Court ruled that this was punitive to white suburbs. More recently, when it accepted the reality of virtually all-black schools (enrolment is 90 per cent black), and sought to turn some into 'Afro-American academies', the courts ruled that the plan infringed desegregation rules.

Detroit was responding to the demands of the rising, post-Civil Rights black middle class, which feels betrayed by the 'broken promise' of integration and would like its children to receive an education more geared to the distinctive needs and wishes of African-Americans. This would stress 'black achievement', history and culture, a more disciplined approach in the classroom, support for confidence and motivation building, and mentoring. And, above all perhaps, it would involve the employment of teachers who can empathise and know how to deal with black children. West Indian parents in London have voiced similar demands.

Since the early-1980s, nearly 400 private Afro-American academies have been established along these lines, and there are fears that, unless the public system can respond to such demands, those black parents who can afford it will opt out in growing numbers. Urban public schools, it is argued, are becoming dumping grounds: "Increasingly, [there] are two tiers of schools in major American cities: free schools for the low-income, and schools costing $1 000 to $10 000 a year for everyone else."[79]

As the proportion of minority children in schools grows – by the end of the decade it is expected to be at least one in six in several European countries, including France and Germany – issues concerning what is 'common' and what is 'distinctive' in relation to different ethnic groups within public education are likely to become more prominent. Matters regarded as private, such as clothing and diet, have become concerns of state, for example the debate in France as to whether Muslim girls should be allowed to wear shalwars in school. Others pose questions of the state itself.

To what extent, if at all, should public funds be used to support the particular educational needs of different groups? In the Netherlands, Muslim and Hindu parents have made use of freedom under the constitution to provide education according to religious creed, by setting up schools which qualify for government subsidies. Conversely, in Britain, where there are a million Muslims, the government has baulked at extending to them the right enjoyed by other religious groups, Christian and Jewish, to set up parochial schools and have running costs and most capital costs met by taxpayers.

Major issues regarding the organisation of education aside, there are a number of immediate and practical measures that might be taken to help minorities, educationally.

Learning the local language

Deficiency in the language of the adopted country is a common handicap for immigrants, particularly new arrivals. It retards educational progress, hinders social interaction, and affects job opportunities. Yet, how many education authorities devote as much attention to tackling this obstacle as they do to teaching a foreign language to indigenous students? How many governments sponsor the publication of commercially-unviable textbooks and other learning resources, such as bilingual dictionaries?

There is a need for the provision of recurring and sustained opportunities as well as for intensive, crash courses. These would cater for both adults and the young, and dovetail with other remedial learning, to bring undereducated immigrants 'up to speed' so that they can compete for well-paid jobs. For young children, opportunities to learn a 'second' language could be created through play.

Where are classes best held? In schools and colleges, in community centres and places used by particular ethnic groups such as mosques, on the premises of non-profit educational associations, or at all of these? And, if the latter, how should opportunities be networked and provision co-ordinated? Should purpose-built language centres be created, equipped for the latest learning technologies and concentrating the scarce bilingual teaching resources available in many minority languages, and which could offer services both to schools and employers?

Maintaining one's own language and culture

Not enough attention is paid, also, to the particular learning needs of different racial and ethnic groups, especially in relation to their own language and culture. Beyond the need for mother-tongue tuition in the early school years, the role of disseminating and promoting 'home' language and culture is left to the minority communities themselves, and many run supplementary schools for the purpose.

However, it is widely recognised that mother tongue proficiency and the self-confidence that comes with pride in one's own cultural heritage not only benefit young people in being able to move easily between their families and communities and the rest of society but also contribute significantly to educational achievement. Children without an adequate sense of their own worth, which must include a positive feeling about the race or ethnic group to which they belong and of which they will be regarded as representatives, will be liable to be perpetually debilitated by what Shelby Steele, in relation to African-Americans, has called inferiority anxiety.[80]

Public education authorities could give support to supplementary schools, particularly in relation to facilities and equipment. In the mid-1980s, the House of Commons committee referred to above concluded that, as far as the public authorities were concerned, the Chinese were "invisible" (there are an estimated 100 000 in London alone). The committee could find not one Chinese on a school governing body, and links between the Chinese and local education authorities were "poor": despite often having difficulty in finding suitable premises, fewer than one in ten of the estimated 60 voluntary Saturday schools, with individual enrolments of up to 900 students, had managed to obtain use of public school premises. The committee recommended that school districts, "where requested, provide premises to mother tongue classes free of charge or at a nominal rent". One city with a constructive attitude is Bradford, England, where the education authority meets the costs of nearly 70 supplementary schools so that Muslim children may learn the Koran after normal school hours.

▷ WASHINGTON DC

Sometimes the mechanical application of regulations can be discouraging to minority, community-based education initiatives. Children of Mine is an after-hours school catering for about 60 African-American 4-17 year-olds in Congress Heights, a poor district of Washington DC. Originally housed in two abandoned apartments, increasing numbers persuaded the school to take over illegal occupancy of the Southeast Neighborhood House, the disused former base for city-funded social services in the district. The school provides help with homework and confidence-building and 'black awareness' sessions, as well as meals, clothing aid, and a summer day-camp. The students sit on upturned boxes and buckets, and the school is funded by the woman who runs it with help from a church. Rather than see the initiative as an opportunity, the city has been trying to evict the school, which it says fails to meet safety regulations.

Raising esteem, giving respect
The physical appearance of educational buildings makes a statement about how society values those who study there. Run-down schools in poor neighbourhoods when contrasted with lavishly appointed ones in middle

class suburbs make a potent impression on students, and do nothing to inspire in them the feeling that education is for them. Also, internal decoration can make a difference in promoting the multicultural ethos of a school.

In his book about the effects of funding disparities between inner city and suburban schools (*Savage Inequalities*), Jonathan Kozol recalls a conversation with a fifth grade African-American girl in Anacostia, a black district of Washington DC. "It's like this," she told him. "The school is dirty. There isn't any playground. There's a hole in the wall behind the principal's desk. What we need to do is first rebuild the school. Another color. Build a playground. Plant a lot of flowers. Paint the classrooms. Blue and white. Fix the ceiling in this room... Make it a beautiful clean building. Make it pretty. Way it is, I feel ashamed... When people come and see our school, they don't say nothing, but I know what they are thinking."[81]

WASHINGTON DC ◁

Links between school and home
Community schools may have especial value in minority and high-immigrant communities, by fostering social interaction, generally, and providing improved opportunities for parents to become involved in the work of schools.

In the Tiergarten district of Berlin, where immigrant children account for about one in three of local schools' enrolment, the education authority decided to create a 'comprehensive' school, rather than a 'streamed' academic, technical or vocational one, in a conscious attempt to promote the integration of immigrants into German society. To this end, the school was also to be a cultural and community centre for the district.

BERLIN ◁

The requirements for the design project said: "The school must take the living conditions and problems of the district as the starting point of its programme. On the one hand, the school must open up to the outside world by including parents, the elderly, the disabled and interested persons with specific skills in both teaching and non-teaching activity, and by incorporating functions organised by non-school groups, such as theatre and music groups, and exhibitions. On the other, the school must also utilise non-scholastic learning locations and sources, in both public institutions and the economic sector, in its programme."

The design of the new Moses-Mendelssohn School, which caters for 600 students aged 10-16, is focused around a central courtyard which opens on to the district's main street. Parents, senior citizens, citizens action groups, voluntary youth organisations, employers, business associations and labour unions were all involved in the planning of the school. The premises are divided into four blocks, the nearest to the street being a 'cultural and community area' which includes an arts centre, a media resource centre, facilities for self-instructional adult learning and for youth recreation, as well as a cafeteria. In addition, public housing authority offices are located on the school site.

Crime and Fear

... one of every five high school students carries a firearm, knife or club on a regular basis. Eight per cent of public school teachers have reported being physically threatened. And all told, approximately three million thefts and violent crimes occur on or near school campuses every year.

Richard Riley, education secretary, announcing the Clinton administration's request to Congress for $175 million over two years to spend on 'schools plagued with violence', June 1993.[82]

School effectiveness research suggests that the management of schools can have a large effect on pupil attitudes, behaviour, attendance and performance and on the likelihood of them drifting into crime. Schools which can offer pupils of all abilities a sense of achievement and which are able to motivate them are likely to reduce the rate of truancy and vandalism.

Evidence to the Inquiry into Juvenile Crime conducted by the House of Commons' Home Affairs Committee, 1993.[83]

Young people are both the most offending and victimised group in society. In the United Kingdom, one in five of all (reported) crimes are committed by those of school age (under 17) and almost half of 'known offenders' are under 21. In the United States, the National Commission on Children reported, in 1991, that, "each year, almost 1.8 million adolescents nationwide are arrested for delinquent offenses, and a growing number of them spend time in jail". Since 1988, teenage boys were more likely to die from gunshot wounds than from all natural causes combined; participation in youth gangs was increasing; and although the proportion of school students using illegal drugs had declined since the early-1980s it remained high.[84] Frequently, young people are victims of other young people, but they also suffer from the effects of living in high crime neighbourhoods and, judged from police and social service reports, increasing levels of sexual and physical abuse at home.

The harsher child and teen environment of the 1990s affects the work of schools. In Toyko, officials complain that increased academic competition is causing greater truancy and bullying.[85] In London, where, according to Roger Graef, "weapon-carrying [is] virtually the norm among teenage boys in many parts of the inner city",[86] the police argue that it is time for a "hearts and minds" campaign in schools to "break the macho violence culture which is particularly appealing to young people".[87] In New York, the director of the city's high schools, Victor Herbert, talks of the emergence of a new breed of young people "who are very reckless, very carefree, and, we believe, very dangerous. There's a real fear among young people about each other," he says.[88]

But it is not realistic to think that schools can be protected completely from what is going on around them: however formidable, defensive measures cannot provide total security. Indeed, turning schools into fortresses may make them more challenging as targets. Also, the costs are prohibitive, and a large share of public resources is already devoted to law enforcement and the penal system. A reasoned approach will weigh the costs of various options against the likely (and known) associated benefits. It will also pursue action across a broad front.

Creating a secure learning environment

Learning can only properly take place in an environment where students and teachers feel safe. Moreover, unsafe schools are likely to founder as institutions. Teachers able to do so will move to other appointments; parents will withdraw their children; and, if a city's public schools as a whole are perceived as dangerous, families may move, or parents send their children to private schools.

Fear can deter participation. 'Being afraid to attend' was cited as one of the six most frequent reasons for failing to complete school classes in a survey of American 14 year-olds and, according to Karl Zinsmeister, eight per cent of urban teenagers miss at least one day of school a month due to fear.[89] The attitudes of colleges towards campus security – and the measures they take to provide it – are of particular importance to women and racial and ethnic minorities, and may affect their choice when applying for places (since passage of the Student Right-to-Know and Campus Security Act, in 1990, American colleges in receipt of public funds must provide to students and staff an annual report on campus crime and its policies for dealing with it).[90] The threat of racist attacks, in particular, may need to be taken into account in the location of new facilities.

Many of the most frequent suggestions for increasing security rely heavily on 'commonsense', and vast sums can be gobbled up with little return except, perhaps, a fleeting boost to public relations.

SECURITY GUARDS AND POLICE
Every day, 300 police officers employed by the school district patrol Los Angeles schools. Yet, in 1993, two people were shot dead in class, and hundreds of guns were taken to school (police in Los Angeles confiscated 765 in 1992). Surveillance can only be sporadic, and costs are high.

METAL DETECTORS

The 'airport approach' of installing detection equipment at the main entrance to school is generally regarded as impractical and ineffective. It slows ingress (30-minute queues at some schools); relies on the feasibility of a single entry; impedes the use of outdoor areas; and weapons can be handed through windows. By turning schools into 'sealed' environments, it discourages parents and restricts the possibility of community use.

Hand-held detectors may provide a measure of deterrence, and can be useful in screening people for entry to particular events, such as after-hours dances and sports fixtures. But, costs will again be high if the equipment is operated by guards employed for the purpose. New York uses detectors for random checks at one-third of its high schools, where they have been welcomed by students and principals. However, it is not yet clear whether the benefits are material as well as psychological.

As an alternative to measures such as these, facility planners could look to 'opportunity reduction' through the improved design and management of schools, including measures aimed at deterrence through surveillance. Schools should support this with curriculum and community initiatives which seek to persuade students to eschew violent and other anti-social behaviour. They might also rethink approaches to exclusion and truancy.

Timothy Crowe is a former director of the National Crime Prevention Institute at the University of Louisville, in Kentucky, who advises education districts planning new schools on what he calls "crime prevention through environmental design". Good design, he says, allows easy surveillance. "We [should] try to spread activities out in such a way that it appears that every part of the school is occupied and somebody is watching it," he told the *New York Times*. Particular attention should be paid to school grounds and parking areas, bathrooms and toilets, and student lockers and corridors.[91]

Transition zones should be clearly demarked to indicate movement from public to semi-public to private space. Space should be redesigned to provide natural barriers between conflicting activities. Formal gathering areas might be included so that other areas become 'off-limits', and those using them will have few excuses for being in the 'wrong' places. Teachers and other school staff thus "assume greater challenging powers through clear spatial definition".

In considering what changes might be made, either to buildings or plans, Crowe recommends an assessment to provide answers to three sets of questions:

Designation. What is the designated purpose of this space? How was it originally intended to be used? How well does the space support its current use and its intended use? Is there conflict?

LIVING IN THE CITY

Definition. How is the space defined? Is it clear who 'owns' the space? Where are its borders? Do social and cultural definitions affect how the space is used? Are the legal or administrative rules for use of the space clearly set out and reinforced in policy? Is the space marked by signs? Does conflict or confusion exist between the designated purpose and definition of the area?

Design. How well does the physical design support the intended function of the space and the type of behaviour that is desired to occur there? Does the physical design conflict with, or impede, the productive use of the space or the proper functioning of the intended activity? Does confusion or conflict exist over the manner in which the physical design is intended to control behaviour?

CLOSED CIRCUIT TELEVISION

Widely used to monitor activity in public places, CCTV is being promoted in British schools as an alternative to security lighting and intruder alarms in providing protection against out-of-hours vandalism, arson and theft. But, school authorities are also being urged to consider "the CCTV option... at the earliest stage of planning", as part of an overall risk assessment.[92]

CCTV promotes deterrence by increasing the likelihood of apprehension (by providing a photographic record); provides surveillance both of people and facilities; and, where a security officer is employed to monitor pictures generated by cameras, offers the possibility of early warning of developing incidents. Coverage can be more comprehensive than is feasible through the use of patrolling guards. The British government, in its advice to schools, concluded that "in certain circumstances" the use of CCTV was "justified and cost effective"; "... evidence suggests that very soon after a CCTV system is installed, there are fewer criminal incidents".

HOT LINES AND PAGERS

DURHAM ◁

In an experiment in Durham, an urban county in the north of England, 21 schools have instituted a 'School Watch' scheme, working with the local police and a telecommunications company. Pagers are used to link teachers and principals with the police, to alert them, and each other, about potential dangers such as suspicious individuals on school premises, threats of vandalism and truanting students.

SCHOOL SECURITY POLICIES

Rules and penalties governing student behaviour are not sufficient: schools should each have a security policy. This would set out the problems faced by the school, in terms of the personal security of its users and as an institution, as well as the integrity of the buildings, equipment and grounds. It would specify the resources (public, corporate and voluntary) and other means available to deal with these problems, and set out the objectives for any planned action so that outcomes may be evaluated.

Protecting educational property

Many of the issues that arise in dealing with personal security in schools also apply to the protection of buildings. So may the use of tactics such as CCTV. However, there are some aspects which are specific to buildings, not least due to the fact that criminal damage to buildings most frequently occurs 'out of hours'.

Since the mid-1980s, the UK government has been collecting annual statistics on the amount and cost of vandalism in relation to buildings, as part of a national crime prevention campaign in schools. Surveys suggest that about 10 per cent of school districts' total maintenance budgets are committed annually to repairing damage caused by arson and vandalism. Costs in big city districts are about three times higher than the national average, with the worst affected being 'areas experiencing social change'.

There are significant variations in the timing of vandalism and arson (weekday evenings and weekends but not school vacations), as well as between individual schools (the same schools are damaged repeatedly) and types of schools (secondary schools are four times more likely to be targets than are primary schools). Schools built in the 1960s and 1970s, with half of their facades glazed, are especially vulnerable. Replacing broken glass accounts for about 60 per cent of vandalism costs, with roofs and fencing distant runners-up. Almost three-quarters of fires occur after 10 pm, and neighbours have been found to be much more effective in raising the alarm than mechanical or electrical means.

The most frequently stolen item from schools is tape recorders. However, video machines and musical instruments account for three-fifths of the value of all stolen goods. Thefts occur during school hours as well as outside them. The greatest risk is when the normal school routine is disturbed; for example, at the end of term, during sports days and when new equipment is delivered and not yet in place.

▷ ENGLAND

The introduction of magnetic 'swipe cards' and electronic readers for students to register their attendance (see above) offers the prospect of wider applications and development of a 'campus card'. One use, copying practice in industry, would be as 'keys' to provide access to restricted rooms and parts of the school building. The system may also be used to record the names of students leaving buildings and the time they left, together with the time they return. This could be applied for fire drills and to police 'internal' truancy – those who absent themselves during the day. Evidence at some schools in England is that electronic registration greatly improves management information, leading to a reduction in truancy and improved punctuality. Little fraudulent use of the cards is reported.[93]

Efforts to combat crime in British schools – including increased expenditure on prevention – appear to be meeting with some success. Overall costs have fallen by nearly 10 per cent since 1987, and the number of 'criminal incidents' decreased by 3.5 per cent in the most recent annual survey.

In issuing guidance on crime prevention to schools, the Department for Education concluded that "prevention measures should fit the nature of the risk. The same measures will not be effective in all situations." However, research has shown that "it was possible to reduce levels of vandalism damage, and to lower the risks of potential damage" by sensitive design which anticipates areas of "robust use", security measures which take into account relative risks of damage, and management methods which can respond quickly to problems. Specifically, the department recommended that schools and districts should take seven steps to prevention. They should anticipate vulnerable areas; design with use in mind; design for robustness; make positive use of casual surveillance; securely store valuable items; deter casual access and intrusion; and foil the determined intruder.

In planning, "... cost and incident information, broken down into comparable units, such as the cost or number of incidents per pupil, can provide a yardstick of cost effectiveness when instituting prevention measures. Such figures will be most useful if kept at an authority wide or even school level, that is, at the level at which decisions about prevention are being taken," said the guidance.[94]

Essentially, schools can adopt one of two approaches. They can opt for case hardening – improving perimeter fencing, providing security lighting, securing vulnerable windows, installing alarms, and similar strengthening measures – or they can go down the road of improved management and community relations, involving the support of teachers and students, and extending the use of buildings to provide self-policing and community support.

ALKMAAR/LEIDEN

Alkmaar and Leiden are cities of approximately 100 000 people about 30 kilometres (19 miles), north and south of Amsterdam, respectively. Schools in both cities had been the recurring target of considerable vandalism, and to tackle this a number of administrative and community approaches have been tried.

Bureaucratic obstacles have been reduced to enable deals to be struck with community groups, so that they obtain free use of school facilities in return for donated work on school grounds. Thus, school surveillance is doubly improved – by the removal of overgrown foliage which provided cover for vandals and by extending the hours in which the building is used.

In Alkmaar, 'for rent' public housing has been built on school premises. The houses are situated so as to afford maximum visibility of the most likely vandalism targets, and a priority-response 'silent alarm' system set up linking residents and local police. Success with two trial houses led to the construction of 12 more in 1990 and a further 14 in 1991. Vandalism costs have been cut by as much as 80 per cent.

Similarly, in Leiden, two schools have been built which incorporate public housing. At one, four homes comprise the building's third (and top) storey. At the other, the school occupies the bottom of four storeys – the top three comprising 18 apartments. Vandalism which occurred at a previous school on one of the sites has not continued, while another benefit in integrating educational and residential facilities was in raising property values, thus lowering the construction costs of the school.

In a third Dutch city, Haarlem, the cost of vandalism to schools and other public buildings has been halved through the implementation of comprehensive crime prevention plans (see case study).

One factor which may contribute to decreased crime is school-based management. Since 1988, British schools have been given increasing powers over their budgets, so that by April 1993 nearly all had control over at least 85 per cent of their running costs, including those related to premises. David Hart, general secretary of the National Association of Head Teachers, says delegated budgets have contributed to a greater awareness of security problems. Increased autonomy has "helped concentrate minds wonderfully". "I think there has been a tremendous push made on the basis that prevention is better than cure."[95]

Alternatives to delinquency

How can education, and the services linked to it, make a more positive intervention in the lives of those young people who regularly truant and drop out of school prematurely? What measures could be taken to discourage deliquent behaviour among those of school age, generally. Broadly, there are five types of action.

EARLY CHILDHOOD PROGRAMMES

These seek to deal with behavioural problems, such as disruptiveness and inability to concentrate, which are likely to threaten progress in school when children are still in kindergarten or the early grades of elementary school. The most successful are school-based, 'multi-agency', and include a high level of involvement by parents. Daycare programmes might require classroom participation by parents on a rotating basis. In some schemes, mothers attend sessions designed to alter parenting behaviour.

YOUTH SUPPORT SERVICES

A variation on the concept of school-based family and health care centres (described above), these involve 'service integration' to bring a wide range of assistance to bear on the problems of 'at risk' youth and their families.

> Comprehensive Youth Service Centers have been set up at nearly 30 New Jersey high schools. Managed by non-profit organisations, public agencies or, sometimes, schools themselves, the centres provide services in relation to primary and preventive health care, mental health and family counselling, substance abuse, family planning and teen parenting, job training and employment guidance, recreation and, in some cases, childcare. The costs of creating the centres are met on a 80:20 basis by state government and local school districts, often with support from business.

NEW JERSEY ◁

CURRICULUM AND COMMUNITY APPROACHES

Drugs education and 'conflict resolution' programmes seek to deal with aspects of students' behaviour that can lead to law-breaking. These are most likely to be effective when extended beyond school – and, thus, to include the use of non-education premises. Parents should be taught about the availability and abuse of drugs, including to recognise signs of use by their children, and professional help should be available through schools. Research on the effectiveness of drugs education programmes in American schools is inconclusive[96], but there is agreement that prevention should be targeted at elementary school pupils, while older students need to be taught ethics (and personal responsibility), rather than 'awareness'.

> Teenagers in the final year of compulsory schooling in Boston take part in a violence prevention project, "which stresses positive ways to deal with anger and arguments, shows how fights start and escalate, and offers non-violent alternatives for the resolution of conflicts". One lesson learnt is that intervention limited to the classroom is not enough: the community has also to become involved, with trained educators carrying the violence prevention curriculum to diverse audiences outside schools – to churches, housing projects, boys' and girls' clubs, neighbourhood health centres and, even, juvenile detention centres.[97]

BOSTON ◁

FLEXIBLE LEARNING

Examples of alternative programmes and schools have already been mentioned (San Diego, St Paul, and in Denmark). Typically, facilities are separate and designed not to resemble ordinary classrooms. Provision may be by public authorities or bought in as a special service, or involve the use of community-based facilities run by voluntary and non-profit organisations. In the latter case, it may be linked with other uses, including out-of-hours programmes and vocational training.

61

Chapeltown and Harehills Assisted Learning Computer School, in Leeds, England, is a school computer centre that provides alternative programmes for "difficult pupils referred by schools" as well as supplementary after-school and weekend computer classes for young people (including on Sundays) and instruction for visiting groups of students during the schoolday – a combination designed to maximise use of the facilities. It also runs classes for community groups, including in computer literacy for women wanting to return to work after child-raising, and is developing a programme in conjunction with the police for students excluded (for disciplinary reasons) from school.

The school is located on the premises of TechNorth, an integrated training and employment centre which provides information technology training and technical support to local firms, including small firms operating from leased enterprise units at TechNorth. Tuition stresses the building of confidence and motivation, and includes mentoring. It is provided by staff at the computer school, liaising on content and assessment with school teachers. The school and TechNorth are funded by the city with support from the European Union, national government and local business. The management committee comprises local people in a district which has a large black population.

Brainard Braimah, who set up and runs the school, attributes its success to high teacher expectation, positive role models for students, and parental involvement.[98] Punctuality and personal appearance are stressed, and the accent is strongly on the acquisition of qualifications. About 400 students attend the school and the same number are on a waiting list, but a strict policy on resourcing applies: during lessons each student must have access to a computer. To involve parents, classes are held for those who want to find out more about what their children are learning.

YOUTH RECREATION

A Carnegie Corporation study in the United States found that about 40 per cent of the out-of-school waking hours of young adolescents aged 9 to 14 was 'discretionary'; it was uncommitted to domestic chores, working for pay, eating, or doing school homework. Almost half of this time was spent watching television. Many "spend virtually all [their] discretionary time without companionship or supervision from responsible adults," noted the Carnegie report.[99]

The issue of 'latch key' children, and the need for after-school programmes as a support for families, has been mentioned. However, many argue that after-school programmes and youth recreational activities also provide a release from peer pressure to join in delinquent behaviour during leisure hours.

School-based activities may be more appropriate than those in the community. As Léon Bing pointed out in her recent study of Los Angeles, neighbourhood clubs are the most common focus for gang formation.[100] Also, participation in youth activities 'in the community' may be hindered by fear, as has been found in British cities: "Young people had a strong sense of territorial boundaries that restricted their movements to certain parts of the estate [public housing project]; physical attack was feared if they moved into another group's territory so that their freedom to choose from the overall range of provision was severely constrained."[101]

In addition, as surveys show, adolescents want a mixture of learning and recreational activities. In Los Angeles, the top requests in a survey carried out shortly after the 1992 riots, all cited by 60 per cent or more of the young people asked, were for activities which helped them: 'to feel better about myself'; to use computers; to learn how to swim; to 'learn about my body and my sexuality'; to learn how to study better; to learn about healthy foods; or which centred on cultural activities. In Britain, counselling and advice facilities were in heavy demand, and "specialist clubs and projects appealing to a particular interest or need were the most successful".

IV

Planning for the City

Life in the great cities... could be improved, and only will be improved, by public action – by better schools with better-paid teachers, by strong, well-financed welfare services, by counselling on drug addiction, by employment training, by public investment in the housing that in no industrial country is provided for the poor by private enterprise, by adequately supported health care, recreational facilities, libraries and police. The question... is not what can be done but what will be paid.
John Kenneth Galbraith, *The Culture of Contentment*. [102]

Large sums have been spent to little apparent effect.
Lord Scarman, report of inquiry into the Brixton riots, in London. [103]

Moving into a post-industrial society

Those who knew Paris, New York or London 30 years ago remember cities very different from those that bear these names today. The markets of Les Halles and Covent Garden still flourished. Longshoremen worked the piers of the Lower West Side and dockers the docks along the banks of the Thames. Tens of thousands earned a weekly wage in warehouses, factories and refineries, and in transport. Even more than downtown, with its palaces of commerce and entertainment, public institutions and bourgeois department stores, the heart of the city lay in the districts of dense tenements and terraced houses where most of its citizens lived – and worked. Beyond, the ring of sedate suburbs seemed almost incidental.

Consumerism, with its stress on individual choice and personal gratification, had yet to overtake older community ties and values. Tourism had not become an industry, and the cities retained a distinctive national character. To shop on Broadway was not the same as shopping on Oxford Street or the Rue de Rivoli; jet passenger services and satellites were only beginning to shrink the physical and cultural space between countries and continents; and, to the majority and the law, 'coloured' people were still 'invisible'. In most respects the cities were not greatly changed from those in which Maurice Chevalier, Charlie Chaplin or the Gershwins had been born three-quarters of a century earlier.

In retrospect, the 1980s may turn out to be the climactic decade, when the forces for change, stimulated by a rare moment of prosperity, gained the momentum to effect a major urban transformation. Observers such as Deyan Sudjic think so. In his book, *The 100 Mile City*, he writes: "...it is clear that the eighties were the decade in which the industrial city finally shook off the last traces of its nineteenth-century self and mutated into a completely new species. Migration and economic development changed it beyond recognition. Technological innovation eliminated traditional industries and scattered new ones in unpredictable places over ever wider distances... Culturally, the successful cities have distanced themselves from their national contexts."[104]

Historically, the 1980s may also come to be seen as the time when it became clear that the industrial model of education was losing its relevance. Longstanding notions of education, as a standardised and tightly regulated system characterised by full-time and obligatory attendance, classroom tuition, narrowly compartmentalised curricula, and testing based on the ability to identify and reiterate 'facts', rather than demonstrate competences, were all being questioned. So was the overall level of attainment by school students compared to what was thought to be necessary for a post-industrial economy.

The most significant educational developments of the decade concerned new information technology and lifelong learning. Both have yet to acquire a critical mass, but when they do – in the coming generation – the effect is likely to be greater than any since the industrial revolution brought the present system into being, or maybe even since Gutenberg invented movable type. If the twentieth century archetype of education was illustrated by rows of young people at desks facing a teacher in front of a blackboard, by the end of the 1980s it was hard to imagine that of the coming century as other than someone, of indeterminate age, interacting with a computer. Accordingly, schools and colleges will cease to be teaching 'factories' and become resource and support centres for learning.

Implementing change

Hitherto, education planners could confidently expect that, in its essentials, the future would mean 'more of the same'; change would be quantitative rather than in kind. Steadily, throughout this century, the numbers of young people engaged in initial education and training have increased, whether in compulsory schooling, pre-schooling and kindergartens, or post-compulsory further and higher education. Fifty years ago, relatively few young people could expect to receive more than about eight years' basic schooling. Now, in many countries, the majority experience at least twice that by the time they leave college. And, for much of the period there was also a 'baby boom'. Planners and architects could generally assume that a new school building would still be in use 40 or more years later, and without any substantial change in its spatial organisation and functions.

Those who seek to restrain the enthusiasm of futurists point out that the existing educational infrastructure is vast, change will therefore take a long time to effect, and most of the facilities of the first quarter of the next century have already been designed and built. They are right. Nevertheless, planning assumptions cannot be as they were. It is not just that new demands for knowledge and skills have emerged, or the creation of new tools for learning: change in all walks of life is faster. The planning horizon is shorter and the environment in which planning takes place is more complex. Implementing and managing change is more complicated and difficult, involving a wider range of participants and new processes. As future needs are uncertain, adaptability and flexibility are required in new building design, and management options should be kept 'fluid' through a strategy which stresses diversity, for example by creating a mixed portfolio of owned and rented property.

The last decade has seen an unprecedented wave of reform sweeping through education, borne in large part on the conviction that knowledge and skills hold the key to future economic prosperity. A succession of reports, such as *A Nation at Risk* in the United States and *Competence and Competition* in the United Kingdom, have argued "a clear link between investment in education and competitive success".[105] In the opening words of the report of the National Commission on Education, in the UK: "In all countries knowledge and applied intelligence have become central to economic success and social well-being."[106] Yet, in spite of the crucial role accorded to education, relatively little attention has been paid by reformers to the implications for the physical environment of learning in implementing change; generally not perceived as significant in helping to improve educational attainment, facilities have tended to be overlooked. Of the 37 key indicators and 77 supporting indicators chosen to measure progress towards the six national Education 2000 goals, proposed by President Bush and adopted by his successor, only one relates to facilities – the proportion of teachers who feel safe in school buildings.

Writing in *Education Week*, Joe Schneider, the deputy executive director of the Southwest Regional Laboratory (one of several federally-funded regional education research and development centres), in California, comments: "Systemic reform requires a lot of a school building. More than most educators realize. And certainly a lot more than educational-policy wonks [advisers] acknowledge, judging from the goals 2000 legislation and the recent report of the independent Commission on Chapter 1 [compensatory education]... Both anticipate massive changes in the way we educate children. But neither says a word about the capability of schools to house the reforms being advocated."[107]

The laboratory carried out a survey of elementary schools in its region and concluded that they faced several deficiencies in seeking to implement change. The list seems almost trivial, but the practical problems were none the less for that.

● The introduction of new curricula and instructional methods was being hindered by inadequate telecommunications and electrical connections, undifferentiated lighting (affecting the use of computers and television screens), and inflexible space (preventing large group instruction). "Only one school [had] a phone in every classroom. Without a telephone line into the classroom, children are not going to be able to receive instruction or curriculum that moves on these lines."

● New methods of assessment required the maintenance of extensive portfolios for each child and space in which to keep student projects, yet schools lacked adequate storage – which also affected the safety of computers, videos and other equipment.

● There was inadequate space for staff development: "None of the spaces teachers now gather in – the cafeteria, student library, or teachers' lounge – is designed to enable teachers to work on computers, view televised instruction, or watch a video. Few are large enough for whole-faculty instruction [that is, involving the entire teaching staff], and most lack the privacy for small-group instruction."

● Despite wanting to increase parental involvement in the work of the school, including in supporting instruction, most lacked appropriate facilities for parents, including a lounge.

● Combining education with on-site health and social services was also restricted by lack of space. One school principal told the laboratory's researchers: "We have no space to house specialists who come to school. They have to work with students out back on the picnic tables."[108]

Redefining government

Governments in the post-industrial society are having to face up to the limits of their powers. The belief, prevalent in the boom years after the Second World War, that the principal problems of economics had been solved and that social scientists could identify the conditions to enable planners to 'engineer' social improvement has all but vanished.

The old measures no longer work; government is experiencing a growing disbelief in the efficacy of its actions, and in some countries the fiscal burden of maintaining public services has become intolerable. New approaches are being adopted which redefine the role of government, mobilise business and community resources towards the meeting of public goals, and provide a more flexible response to the demands and opportunities arising from increasingly rapid change.

Faced with a huge portfolio of responsibilities and lacking the resources to cope with them, cities in the 1980s sought first to use established means to assert control. They raised taxes, reduced the growth rate in running costs, made real cuts in capital spending, discontinued services, increased fees and service charges, froze staff hiring and laid off employees. By using these defensive tactics they hoped to maintain the status quo. However, not only did this provide an unfavourable context for any major initiative to reverse urban fortunes, the tactics sometimes misfired.

> When Philadelphia raised taxes 19 times in 10 years it ended up with no more money in real terms than when it began. In the process it lost an estimated 130 000 jobs and one in 16 of its residents. Half of its taxpayers had become classified as 'low income', and the deficit on the 1992 city budget of $2.3 billion was approaching 10 per cent, when it was realised a new approach had to be adopted. City government would be 'downsized' and the focus switched from being 'services-led' to financial management.

PHILADELPHIA ◁

The shift taking place in the role of government has been characterised by David Osborne and Ted Gaebler, in their influential book *Reinventing Government,* as one of from 'rowing' to 'steering'. They quote the mayor of St Paul, George Latimer, in his 1986 'State of the City' address, in which he said: "City government will have to make some adjustments and in some ways redefine its traditional role. I believe the city will more often define its role as a catalyst and facilitator. The city will more often find itself in the role of defining problems and then assembling resources for others to use in addressing those problems... City government will have to become even more willing to interweave scarce public and private resources in order to achieve our community's goals."[109]

In education, the move towards 'steering' is being given added impetus by the fact that, in many parts of the developed world, the compulsory school system has been contracting, due to decreased birth rates, while the voluntary areas – pre-schooling, industrial training, and higher and adult education – are growing. Increasingly, the achievement of public goals for education falls beyond the purview of government. Also, as we have seen, it is no longer as practicable as it once was to regard education in isolation from its social context.

> In England and Wales, local government control of education has been considerably reduced in favour of a combination of greater central powers, to secure a national framework and standards, on the one

ENGLAND/WALES ◁

hand, and increased institutional autonomy on the other.[110] In effect, the previously all-important middle layer of administration has been diminished in a move to a flatter management structure: the local education authorities no longer run schools as such, rather they have a strategic role for the provision of adequate educational services in their locality.

All English and Welsh schools now have control over at least 85 per cent of their recurrent expenditure (running costs), encompassing the purchase of books, materials, equipment and repairs as well as the hiring of teachers and other staff. In addition, schools can now choose, on a majority vote of parents, to receive funding direct from national government rather than through local school boards; about a thousand schools have 'opted out' in the last three years. New categories of schools have been created which are entirely self-governing as charitable trusts (see the case study on city technology colleges), while all colleges in the post-16 sector of education have been given corporate status, receiving public funding through a new national agency instead of local government.

Collaboration and partnership

Changes in the role and responsibilities of government, and the need to enlist wider support in pursuit of public goals, are giving impetus to new approaches to planning. These reflect the need to involve others in the process, through partnership with the private and voluntary sectors, as well as greater collaboration and co-ordination between and within government.

INTER-GOVERNMENTAL COLLABORATION

Different levels of government – local, regional, national and international (such as the European Union) – collaborate to facilitate new developments. This may involve strategic funding, as part of a specific programme, on a project basis, or as part of a comprehensive redevelopment scheme. Contributions may be in cash or other resources (land, property, personnel, etc.), and funding may be leveraged ('challenge grants' or 'matching funds') and temporary ('catalytic' or 'pump priming').

Facilitation at the local level involves the identification of funding opportunities and the packaging of proposed developments in such a way as to attract partners. Often, these partners will include business, and schemes may offer opportunities for neighbouring (education) authorities to collaborate. Reflecting their shared provenance, new facilities will cater for several clients – in the public sector, business, community and voluntary organisations, as well as individuals. Ownership and management may lie outside, or jointly with, government; nevertheless, the existence of the facilities, and the opportunities they offer, will need to be taken into account by education facility planners.

INTRA-GOVERNMENTAL CO-ORDINATION

Different departments and agencies of (city) government co-ordinate their efforts. But overcoming administrative pigeonholing in a system-oriented organisation, as local government has been and largely still is, can mean surmounting major obstacles of resourcing, ethos and accountability; even within education, there may be separate departments and agencies (for schools, vocational and technical education, higher education, and adult and community education) which have a history of not speaking to each other. One tactic is to work through third parties or specially-created, freestanding organisations. These can work more flexibly and may be able to access additional resources, although democratic control may be lessened.

In the late-1980s, the UK government established a national network of training and enterprise councils to co-ordinate business support initiatives at the local level. Following the model of private industry councils in the United States, the councils are business-led in terms of corporate representation on their boards of management and act as agents for a variety of government-funded programmes and services. These include Youth Training for 16-19 year-olds not in full-time education or employment, Training For Work (for the long-term adult unemployed), and 'work-related' education in colleges. In addition, the councils have a local co-ordinating role in the achievement of national education and training targets, through committees known as 'education strategic forums', and the development of school-business partnerships.

> The Quest Centre, in an industrial district of Greater Manchester, MANCHESTER ◁
> England, is not part of the local education service, nor of the
> employment service or the economic development office. It is a 'one
> stop shop' funded by government but run, and additionally supported,
> by the local training and enterprise council. It provides "a resource [for]
> employment, training and education opportunities and a base for
> outreach into the community by other agencies" – including the local
> education authority and colleges. Functions include: careers and
> education information (a library and database), counselling (including
> on education and training routes, qualifications and student finance
> options), and referral to particular courses (in liaison with providers).
> It also runs a clearing house for job vacancies, an 'ethnic minority
> business service', and provides business counselling on premises,
> markets, loans, land development and other aspects of enterprise.

CORPORATE SUPPORT FOR PUBLIC SCHOOLS

Business resources are recruited to public education in a number of ways, including for the development of new programmes, the provision of work experience, and the contribution of management expertise in the running and organisation of schools.[111]

In Newark, New Jersey, the telephone company AT&T co-funds with the city an alternative school for high school drop-outs, and in Miami corporate funding has been obtained to build new public elementary schools as 'satellite learning centers'. These are located on company premises and provide education for the five-to-eight year-old children of employees of the donor organisations – an insurance firm and the city's airport authority.

In Memphis each of the city's 157 schools has had at least one corporate sponsor since the Adopt-a-School scheme started in 1983. However, the city does not encourage straight gifts of money or new equipment, and decisions on adoption are not taken by company directors or executives alone. Instead, they must have the widespread support of employees, whose involvement as volunteers is the keystone of the scheme. Typically, they contribute their own time in landscaping, repairing and decorating school premises, while their firms give them time off to provide teaching support and mentoring. The companies also engage in fundraising for new facilities and equipment, and, collectively, they contribute unwanted business equipment and furniture to a warehouse run by the school district, and from which schools can select items of use.

Although the private sector is often involved in supplying equipment to schools, it is less common for business to be involved directly in the provision or management of facilities. However, in 1993, a British education minister, referring to the private sector's contribution in sponsoring the creation of city technology colleges, observed: "There are also cases where land and buildings are made available as part of a development gain or a redevelopment package, or as joint ventures between a school and a firm. Sometimes specialist facilities are leased from a commercial firm, for example sports facilities and science labs. Some school premises are sometimes leased to private companies, where the premises are now too big for the school. We think, however, that this is relatively underdeveloped... We are talking of what is potentially a very big market... a building stock valued at £40 billion [$60 billion], with an annual capital investment programme approaching £0.75 billion."[112]

CONTRACTING OUT PUBLIC SERVICES

Strictly speaking, the contracting of private companies and institutions to provide public services need not entail partnership any more than the usual customer-supplier relationship. However, because government has legal responsibilities for education provision, is accountable for outcomes as well as the use of public monies, and publicly-owned property may be involved, authorities tend to perceive these arrangements as 'partnerships'.

Contracting out may involve the delivery of education on private premises or the creation of privately-run and equipped learning centres within schools (perhaps offering new services which might otherwise have been provided by the city), or it may entail the purchase of management services.

In Massachusetts, one school district has contracted with a private university to take over the entire management of its schools, while, in 1992, Baltimore signed a $140 million five-year deal whereby a private firm, Education Alternatives, will operate nine of its 177 schools.

Education Alternatives Inc. has invested about $1 million and spent two years in developing its approach to pedagogics and school management. The firm's 'Tesserat' system involves one teacher and an instructional intern working with each group of 30 students. Each student has a personal education plan, and learning methods emphasise self-instruction using computers and books, and 'real-life' project work.

BALTIMORE ◁

In the school year 1992/93 the company received $5 549 for each of the 4 800 students at the eight elementary schools and one middle school taking part. This is the average amount the city spends. About $6 million has been spent by the firm on putting computers, fax machines, phones and copiers into classrooms, and in rewiring the schools, and the intention is to increase from $60 to $150 per student the amount spent annually on educational supplies. Maintenance is sub-contracted to another company, with the mission to reduce costs and raise efficiency, although an initial $240 000 has been spent in 'fixing up' the schools.

Writing in *Education Week*, Peter Schmidt says Education Alternatives has not yet "demonstrated that it can profitably run public schools at their current funding levels", but its strategy is "to free up money to improve education by trimming about 25 per cent of school expenditures, especially in such waste-prone areas as maintenance, secretarial services, food preparation, purchasing, and administration".[113]

An end of first year report praised graffiti-free and clean premises and the influx of new equipment. Parents were enthusiastic, although there have been complaints about the elimination of subjects such as music and Spanish; the approach is a technology-intensive 'back to basics' which does not allow scope for an extended curriculum or the community use of premises. Teacher unions remained sceptical, arguing that the company is simply using the city's schools, teachers and curriculum to turn a profit. The city's mayor is awaiting improved academic test scores; but the schools superintendent is reported to want the scheme expanded, to enable children taking part to continue to do so at high school.

Apart from contracting out, education authorities are extending their commercial arrangements through buying in more services and by funding additional provision through user fees. Facilities for schools are being rented or leased; public money is used to buy places in private schools; and extended day programmes may be funded, at least in part, through charges levied on parents.

WORKING WITH THE VOLUNTARY SECTOR

Some countries have long traditions of public support for schools run by voluntary organisations. Parochial ('voluntary aided') schools in Britain, owned and run by religious organisations, have their running costs and most of their capital costs met by government, providing they meet criteria on curriculum and standards, including those relating to buildings. In the Netherlands, there is constitutional provision for voluntary organisations (and individuals) to set up public schools whose costs are met by government.

Beyond school, extensive support is given to the voluntary sector in providing learning opportunities through adult educational associations, such as the Swedish *studieförbund*, as well as youth organisations, and pre-school and play group associations. In Austria, *volkshochschulen* provide neighbourhood adult learning opportunities; the schools are privately run but city authorities own the buildings and pay about one-third of the running costs.

Increasingly, new types of education are being launched which are publicly funded, have government-set objectives, and may connect with the public system, but are managed by non-governmental organisations, including in the voluntary sector. For example, in Denmark, production schools for 16-19 year-olds are government-funded but independently managed; they may be housed on school premises or elsewhere.

SPAIN

Workshop schools (*Escuelas-taller*), set up in Spain to help reduce youth unemployment, provide craft training in the area of heritage conservation, for example the renovation of monuments. The course comprises a six-month introductory element, carried out on-site, and two years' vocational training for which the practical component is a restoration project. Started with a dozen schools in 1985, by the end of the decade numbers had grown to more than 400 schools and 30 000 students. The scheme is funded by the Spanish Ministry of Employment, with extra support from the European Union. Projects are run by non-profit institutions, community organisations and private companies.

In the Netherlands, 'Alida de Jong schools' have been set up to help women aged over 25, especially those with children and no previous vocational training, to get jobs. Begun in Utrecht, in 1984, the scheme was developed by the Union of Housewives (*Vrouwenbond*) and has since spread to other Dutch cities. Courses concentrate on information technology and enterprise skills, and are run over ten months. Hours fit in with those of elementary schools and crèche facilities are provided. There are no fees, and costs are met by the national government and the European Union.

NETHERLANDS ◁

Individual local voluntary organisations (as opposed to those belonging to national or regional associations) can also play a useful role in supplementing the work of public schools and colleges. Often, however, they are constrained by shoestring budgets, problems with premises and a lack of technical 'know-how'. Partnership with government can help ease these difficulties, and may result in substantial additional resources being recruited to the community.

Finally, major non-profit (or charitable) foundations can be an important source of financial support for education initiatives. In the United States they fund research and demonstration projects (the 'charter' initiative in Philadelphia has received $16 million since 1988 from one foundation) and have underwritten the development of new designs for schools. In New York, a non-profit organisation is raising money in the private sector to help fund the creation of new public schools; it provides grants to a wide variety of organisations to develop plans for the ('New Visions') schools, among them universities, libraries, and historical associations.

WORKING WITH THE COMMUNITY
Individual schools and colleges form partnerships with community organisations to increase public support for their work, to help open up educational facilities to wider use, and to access others' premises in delivering education on an outreach basis.

Several municipalities in the Netherlands have developed an approach, known as 'community control', which seeks to combine a co-ordinated response by government departments and agencies with community team-building, in a concerted effort for neighbourhood improvement. One focus has been improving the physical environment of schools by reducing the effects of crime (see the Haarlem case study).

Parents as partners

Another type of collaboration is that between schools and parents. Some schools have longstanding and beneficial relationships with parents, formalised in parent-teacher associations and, less often, 'friends organisations', which also include other supporters. Parents may, in addition, have a formal, even statutory, role in school government, electing representatives to the school governing body; and in countries such as Denmark and the Netherlands there is a tradition of parents founding and running their own schools with public financial support.

Fund-raising for books and materials, equipment and facilities is a way in which parents frequently seek to enhance the environment in which their children learn and develop as individuals. They may also contribute towards curriculum enrichment, financing study visits and paying for supplementary lessons, as well as extra-curricular activities, notably sports and the performing arts; and they may volunteer their labour to carry out maintenance and repair, decoration and landscaping projects.

Strong parental involvement has often been noted as an important indicator of school effectiveness: schools that do well educationally tend to be those where parents take an active interest in their children's progress and complement the work of school with learning and encouragement at home. Equally, children who succeed at school tend to come from homes where education is valued and pressure is put upon children to do well, and to survive at school.

There are signs that the nature of home-school liaison is changing. More parents appreciate not so much that education holds the key to better jobs and higher earnings, which they always knew, but that the economy has less and less to offer those who do not have educational qualifications. Increased parental concern about their children's 'life chances' is reflected in greater activism and a demand to be consulted, not merely informed, by schools.

▷ CHICAGO   Proposals in the late-1980s to give parents a greater say in the running of schools were often criticised on the grounds that too few would come forward for procedures to be democratically effective. Yet, when Chicago created school councils 17 000 people stood for election, and the turn out was higher than in elections for the city's school board.

Research on home-school links, in Scotland, has concluded that parents have clear views on what they expect schools to be like, in terms of organisation and ethos, and they "increasingly expect to be brought into the picture and to be treated as a partner in the child's education".[114] Based on these and similar findings, there would appear to be a number of implications as regards facilities in creating effective parent-school partnerships.

● Parents expect schools to be welcoming, socially and physically. They should be accessible, and not cut-off by fortress-like security arrangements. There should be signs to show visitors the way. Foyers and reception areas should be inviting, and school offices conveniently located.

● The presence of litter and graffiti, or general lack of repair, tend to be equated by parents with the standards of pupils' work, behaviour and staff management. Dirty and poorly-kept schools are bad for student pride and teacher morale, but they are also dispiriting for parents, and, as such, are likely to deter involvement.

● Parents want information about their children's progress, and they also want to know – and to be consulted on – what the school is doing and why, in terms of the curriculum, timetabling, assessment, and discipline. But they don't want to be talked at in large information-giving meetings: they prefer small group discussions and one-to-one meetings with teachers – ideally in settings which do not emphasise the territoriality and status of professionals. Yet, many schools lack informal and 'neutral' spaces for such meetings.

● Workshops which take them through curriculum materials or aspects of the school's work are appreciated by parents, provided they engage them at their own level. However, schools also often lack rooms suitable for study and instructional use by adults.

● Those parents whose involvement may be most desired, to benefit underachieving or 'at risk' students, are often the least likely to have an active relationship with the school, and they may feel daunted by the apparent confidence and cliquishness of those taking part in parent-teacher association activities. Ways to reach such parents include through providing additional services - crèches and facilities for mothers-and-toddlers groups - and the location on school premises of health and social services offices. Alternatively, schools could use community centres to run regular parent surgeries and mobile units to tour residential areas, providing access to information and advice (and possibly linked to library services, adult education, or child immunization programmes).

● Parents who work as volunteers in schools require a lounge or social area in which to relax, keep personal belongings, and over which they feel a sense of ownership.

● Community use of school buildings can lead to a considerable increase in parental involvement in the work of schools.

The need for innovation

It is not enough simply to increase the number of 'players' in the planning process or to create new mechanisms for consensus building and resource mobilisation, the ethos of planning must also change: the pace of change implies that planners should seek to anticipate developments, rather than react to them. Education authorities need to develop cultures – ways of thinking and behaving – that foster innovation. But what does this mean in terms of management?

Until recently, the role of public education was relatively straightforward. Local education authorities built and ran schools (for the young) and colleges (for older teenagers). Regional or national authorities financed universities, which largely ran themselves. And, in some countries, school districts ventured into the provision of youth recreation, adult education, and pre-school facilities. Mostly, these institutions got on with their job, which they perceived as teaching or research or both, hoping for as little 'outside' interference as possible.

If asked, education officials at city hall probably thought of themselves as administering a system – an education service – that was distinct from the rest of local government, and with which links were often tenuous (in the USA, in particular, school boards have been constituted as entirely separate entities with their own sources of income and elected officials). Authority was hierarchical, and the system managed by regulation. Officials were problem-focused, intent on resolving operational difficulties and demands, while outcomes were measured in qualifications and graduations. When something new appeared, such as computer technology, the instinct was to use it to do what had always been done but in a different way, rather than to do something different. Most demands on the system came from the professionals who ran it, rather than 'users'.

'Innovation', as championed by management theorists such as Peter Drucker, stands most of these practices on their head. It calls for a responsiveness to developments in society as a whole, rather than to needs as defined by the service. It promotes experimentation over regimentation, and favours devolved responsibility and workplace initiative. Crucially, it also makes the satisfaction of user needs the touchstone of performance.[115]

Drucker emphasises that innovation is not about looking for the 'biggie' – the single development with a revolutionising impact – but, rather, the exploitation of change, usually in quite modest and specific ways. It is less about breakthroughs than the constant teasing open of opportunities, and it has little to do with 'flashes of genius': at least 90 per cent of innovation is 'purposive', and may be planned and organised. A practice of innovation is possible, he says, and can be learned. It involves the "organised search for changes" and the "systematic analysis of the opportunities such changes offer". This requires good management information – both about an organisation's own performance and external trends; an environment that facilitates the exploration of ideas, the interplay of different expertise and experience, and the ready testing of solutions; and practitioners who are well-educated and creative.

Whether the concept of 'customers' can be applied meaningfully in the public sector is a matter of debate. Some believe it can, and are adopting quality techniques and systems such as total quality management.[116] Others say customer satisfaction in education is facile. The benefits are too widely spread to be attributed to particular groups, such as parents or employers, and they extend too far into the future to be properly assessed. Besides, outcomes ought to be substantive and objectively determined: the issue is not whether students are 'satisfied' but whether they are educated.

Nevertheless, the techniques and organisational requirements of 'innovation' may help planners to be more creative in managing change. In such an approach, they would:

● Examine process needs – as indicated by demographic and economic trends, so that developments such as increasing surplus space in schools and the rising demand for educational provision from women seeking to return to the labour market may be anticipated.

● Consider objectives rather than system needs.

● Analyse what works and build on success, rather than being problem-oriented.

● Listen to 'customers' – not only in determining provision but in finding out how to improve it. What kind of after-school activities would be attractive to young people of different ages, and where would they best be located? Which adults will 'return to learn' in schools and which prefer courses to be run at community centres – and why?

● Understand new technologies, so that their potential is fully exploited, rather than being used merely as a replacement for old methods.

● Exploit incongruities: instead of asking why something isn't happening as it 'ought', perceive apparent failure as an opportunity. For example, is dropping out a call for the increased enforcement of attendance or a demand for alternative forms of education?

● Monitor the unexpected. Why do some things happen when they 'shouldn't', and how can this be capitalised upon?

UNITED KINGDOM ◁

In Britain, black teenagers as a group underachieve at school, so it might be expected that more than average would take the opportunity of the end of compulsory attendance to drop out. In fact, proportionately more black 16 year-olds continue in full-time education than do their white counterparts. Black youths get more support for continuing from their families, but research also shows that key factors in determining staying on are that the British system allows 16 year-olds to retake basic qualifications by transferring to the more adult environment of a college and that a wide range of vocational curricula and qualifications become available, which are seen by young blacks as especially important in enhancing their competitiveness in a racially-biased jobs market.[117] An unwitting consequence of the 'break at 16' is that college and university enrolment among British blacks is high – in fact, considerably higher than that of British whites.

The planning triangle

In 1961, when city government was engaged in massive urban clearance and redevelopment projects, Jane Jacobs, in her book *The Death and Life of Great American Cities*, made a famous assault on the then fashionable assumptions of planners.

"There is a wistful myth that if only we had enough money to spend – the figure is usually put at a hundred billion dollars – we could wipe out all our slums in ten years, reverse decay in the great, dull, grey belts that were yesterday's and the day-before-yesterday's suburbs, anchor the wandering middle class and its wandering tax money, and perhaps even solve the traffic problem," she wrote.

"But look what we have built with the first several billions: Low-income projects that become worse centers of delinquency, vandalism and general social hopelessness than the slums they were supposed to replace. Middle-income housing projects which are truly marvels of dullness and regimentation, sealed against any bouyancy or vitality of city life. Luxury housing projects that mitigate their inanity, or try to, with a vapid vulgarity. Cultural centers that are avoided by everyone but bums, who have fewer choices of loitering than others. Commercial centers that are lack-luster imitations of standardized suburban chain-store shopping. Promenades that go from no place to nowhere and have no promenaders. Expressways that eviscerate great cities. This is not the rebuilding of cities. This is the sacking of cities."[118]

Instead of 'top down' intervention and socially-engineered solutions, Jacobs argued for a greater understanding of how cities actually function: what makes some squares and open spaces well-used and others hang-outs for derelicts; why some streets are secure while others attract crime; why old-fashioned neighbourhoods encourage community life while new projects and high-rise blocks foster alienation and fear. Only through the study of how cities work, rather than how planners think they ought to work, she argued, is it possible "to learn what principles of planning and what practices in rebuilding can promote social and economic vitality in cities, and what practices and principles will deaden these attributes".

A like attention to untidy and particular realities has also been advocated in dealing with social problems. "If we want to understand what is happening to those at the bottom of American society," says Christopher Jencks, "we need to examine their problems one at a time, asking how each has changed and what has caused the change. Instead of assuming that the problems are closely linked to one another, we need to treat their inter-relationships as a matter of empirical investigation... Exaggerating the correlations among social problems can have political costs. Portraying poverty, joblessness, illiteracy, violence, unwed motherhood and drug abuse as symptoms of a meta-problem, such as the underclass, encourages people to look for meta-solutions. We are frequently told, for example, that piecemeal reform is pointless and that we need a comprehensive approach to the problems of the underclass."[119]

The lure of the big solution is still seductive, but, as Lord Scarman, in his inquiry report into the causes and events of the Brixton riots in London in 1981, wrote: "Large sums have been spent to little apparent effect... A 'top-down' approach to regeneration does not seem to have worked." What was needed, instead, he said, was "an effective co-ordinated approach to tackling inner city problems", a greater involvement of the private sector in regeneration, and for "local communities [to] be more fully involved in the decisions which affect them... in planning, in the provision of local services, and in the management and financing of specific projects".[120]

This trinity – government, business, and the community – comprises more than a list of prospective partners in regeneration, however. It also represents three rival philosophies of action: intervention ('government and experts know best'), laissez-faire ('markets know best'), and empowerment ('people – users and residents – know best'). Between these approaches are played out the questions of 'who plans?', 'who determines objectives?', 'who manages?' and 'who funds?' Finding a pragmatic point within the triangle, at which the practical benefits of collaboration are optimised, is one of the difficulties facing planners. It requires an appreciation, unencumbered by ideological considerations, of what each partner does best.

What government can do

In 'reinventing' government there is the danger that its role may be undervalued, while that of its erstwhile partners is overplayed. In some reform proposals business appears almost as ersatz government, with institutionised funding and management roles in the pursuit of public goals. Similarly, as David Robins has remarked about empowerment in relation to community schemes, "...politicians can often sound blithely optimistic about the organisational resources of poor neighbourhoods".[121]

Business has an operational, commercial interest in the existence of a well-educated and trained workforce, and it may be willing to support schools and colleges for philanthropic (and tax) reasons, but any effort it makes on behalf of the community at large must, necessarily, be marginal to its essential purpose. Organisations in the voluntary sector, too, have their own agendas, which may or may not coincide with public goals. Neither voluntarism nor corporate action can satisfy the need for public services which are coherently-planned, comprehensive in scope, and continuously provided. By contrast, one of the main advantages of extra-governmental contributions is that they can enable something specific to be done in the short term that might not happen otherwise.

Ted Kolderie believes business should more often resist the blandishments of government, preferring instead to argue the case for more action by government itself. In his article *Education That Works: The Right Role for Business*, he says: "Business should be tougher. When approached for support, executives should ask the central question, 'If these things are so important (donating computers... recognizing outstanding teachers... helping pass a law extending the school year...), why aren't they important enough for the system to do itself? Why are they done only when we finance them?' If business were thinking strategically, it would be happy to see that schools get opportunities and incentives to innovate on their own."[122]

Robins says: "The idea of... legislation to help communities control their own affairs counts for little when people are busy surviving from one crisis to another. Election-campaign pledges to improve the quality of neighbourhood life have a limited impact when the desire of many residents is to move out as quickly as possible. [What is needed] is less rhetoric about regeneration – schemes, projects, programmes, initiatives, challenges, ventures – and more practical help from government, on a large scale, over a sustained period of time, to achieve modest, incremental gains such as improving the quality of childcare and educational attainment, and raising the incentives for young people to work, to train for jobs, or set up in business on their own."

The adoption of market-led approaches and increased institutional autonomy do not diminish, but rather reinforce, the need for effective government. Markets do not function perfectly. Often they fail to take into account wider benefits (beyond the returns to a particular firm); they may not handle risk adequately, for example in financing adults wishing to invest in the acquisition of new skills; high development costs can inhibit innovation; and decisions may be flawed due to a lack of (costly) information. Government has a vital role in helping markets to be more efficient as well as in providing those things that markets cannot.

Devolved responsibility to individual schools and colleges and centralised reform initiatives are not mutually exclusive. "Systematic reform needs elements of decentralization and central control," says Chris Barnham, in his study of how Chicago and Pittsburgh are tackling education reform.[123] "Control of the school budget, school management and detailed curriculum development properly belong at the individual school level. But there are things which schools alone cannot and should not do; some agency beyond the school must offer a framework of guidance and support to schools, ensure their accountability, reward success and take remedial action in cases of failure... The real questions are what, in the interests of more effective schools, should be decentralized, and what role, in a system of largely autonomous schools, should be retained by school districts?"

Nor does institutional empowerment necessarily result in increased creativity in educational planning. In theory the devolution of power to individual schools enables them to 'cut through the red tape' and become more flexible in their arrangements, enhancing their responsiveness to the needs of students, parents, employers and others in the community. However, in practice, it can result in a narrowing of focus to 'core' tasks, especially where performance criteria are restricted to these tasks.

> Evidence on the implementation of school-based management in the United Kingdom suggests that it has served to concentrate more power in the hands of headteachers (principals). Reports by Her Majesty's Inspectors and the Brookings Institution give many examples of schools where energetic and creative headteachers have 'made things happen'.[124] In some cases repairs have been carried out more quickly and cheaply; and sponsorship has been obtained for new facilities and improvement schemes. However, as we have seen, rules governing the delegation of budgets, intended to provide for accountability in public spending, have worked against the use of schools for after-hours schemes. Also, in the long term, there is the risk that devolved authority will lead to a decline in facility standards and fragmentation of the overall educational infrastructure.

UNITED KINGDOM ◁

The role of government cannot be reduced to that of merely a strategist and facilitator: it must provide leadership, expertise in specialised and technical aspects of education (including facilities planning and management), as well as services which are best carried out and can only be guaranteed on a city-wide or broad basis, such as the professional development of teachers, provision for children with disabilities, and adult education. Also, it must ensure that education is adequately resourced. Without these things the ability of schools to perform well, regardless of their degree of autonomy, will be severely hampered.

Following a survey of more than 70 schools and nearly 50 youth clubs, colleges and adult education centres in depressed districts in seven English cities, Her Majesty's Inspectors concluded: "Schools, and other educational institutions, can do more to improve their own effectiveness... But most schools in these disadvantaged areas do not have within themselves the capacity for sustained renewal. The rising tide of national education reform is not lifting these boats."[125]

"It is not a case of expecting schools and other services merely to try harder, to import ideas that have appeared to work elsewhere or to offer short-term funding for projects. A systematic programme of improvement is required; but the unique blend of difficulties, and also of strengths, in each institution and each locality means that strategies have to be tailored to need, well managed, and sustained over long periods of continuing educational change... The evidence of the survey is that the most successful initiatives occur when a particular need is precisely identified, strategies are designed and resources deployed specifically to meet it, and sustained structures and processes are put in place."

What good government requires

"Life in the great cities... could be improved, and only will be improved, by public action...," says the economist John Kenneth Galbraith. Only government can strike a balance between the interests of individuals and groups and the needs of society as a whole. It alone can ensure an adequate physical infrastructure, the continuity and stability of services, and the pursuit of social cohesion and equity. But, as cities grow, existing government arrangements may become unequal to these tasks. There is the risk that metropolitan areas will fragment into extremes of wealth, become more wasteful in the way they use resources, and, ultimately, cease to be effective in offering a place where people and those who employ them want to be: these are problems now faced by many American cities.

The process that most characterises suburban growth in the United States is privatisation. People increasingly want the directness and immediacy they experience as consumers, rather than what they see as the obligations and uncertain benefits of membership in something as unexclusive as a city. Ironically, they want a more, not less, controlled environment, but one where space and facilities are privately-managed and, thus, a matter of consumer 'choice'. Taxes must be kept low to protect purchasing power and enable residents to buy services not provided (or only at a basic level) collectively through the auspices of government. One of the motives for the flight to the suburbs is to escape the jurisdiction of city government – and, often, that of the city school board, in particular.

Increasingly, the suburban landscape consists of corporate-owned and run shopping malls, which, unlike public streets, do not allow a general right of access: users should have a legitimate purpose and behave appropriately. The premises are privately policed, and profitable shops can be told to leave if they no longer complement the marketing profile desired by the owners. Much the same is true for offices and factories on privately-developed and managed business parks. Residential communities, built and run by property management companies, provide highly regulated living environments with their own recreational and service facilities, security forces and private roads.

The obverse of privatisation is exclusion, so that in Atlanta, a city which has tripled in population to three million, covering five counties, in a little over 20 years, the downtown area adjacent to the old working class districts and at the centre of the public transport system now has only one major department store and no cinemas or theatres. The bus and rapid rail system is excluded by suburban voters from the two most prosperous and rapidly-growing counties (in part deliberately to keep out 'poor blacks', but with the added effect of denying those without cars access to jobs). Public schools have become virtually 'resegregated' by race. The mayor of the City of Atlanta now represents only 13 per cent of the metropolitan population.

In the United States, the strong tradition of self-determination and distrust of government has produced a virtually unreformable plethora of local elected bodies – more than 80 000 nationwide. Metro Atlanta, for example, comprises not only five counties but, within them, more than 40 cities, the smallest with only 800 inhabitants, and more than 60 separate public police forces. Nationally, there are 15 300 school districts, with a median enrolment of 2 900 students and an average population of 16 250. Leaving aside the administration of elementary schools, which is sometimes carried out at a very local level, these figures are much lower than in other developed countries. (For example, the average population of the 54 Greek prefectures is 190 000; of the county and city secondary school districts in Denmark 321 000; of the 129 local education authorities in Britain 438 000; and of the 17 'autonomous communities' in Spain 2.3 million.)

But neither inefficiency nor lack of specialised expertise are the most striking aspects of American local government as regards education: it is the heavy reliance on local tax revenue and the absence of adequate mechanisms at state or higher level to iron out the differences between rich and poor districts. Still less is there an attempt, as in other developed countries, to equalise inputs: to fund schools according to educational need and allowing for the difficulty of their task owing to the varying social circumstances of parents and students.

The result is wide disparities in resourcing between inner city and suburban schools (and, thus, between predominantly black and predominantly white schools). In his book examining these 'savage inequalities', Jonathan Kozol estimates, for example, that in 1989 "any high school class of 30 children in Chicago received approximately $90 000 less... than would have been spent on them if they were pupils of a school such as New Trier High [in suburban Winnetka]".[126] He quotes John Coons' conclusion that providing radically different education on the basis of governmental boundaries and residence "[has] combined to make the public school into an educator for the educated rich and a keeper for the uneducated poor".[127]

Overcoming barriers between neighbourhoods, income groups and races is not easy, and some of the tactics used – notably busing in the United States – have proved counter-productive (others, such as magnet schools, have been more successful). However, as David Rusk, a former mayor of Albuquerque, has shown in his study of 500 American cities, where a city has managed to expand its boundaries "to follow its suburbs and keep the middle class... within the city, paying its taxes, running its government and solving its problems", the average per capita income of inner areas exceeds that of the outer suburbs, and both areas "do well".[128] Where a city has not expanded, the 'central city' declines dramatically.

Good government requires a political jurisdiction large enough to enable a city to develop the expertise and efficiency to provide up-to-date and effective services. It also needs adequate funding – that is, tax revenues – and the democratic authority to act and enforce change, if necessary. None of these things are possible without a common sense of purpose and the political leadership to foster it.

REFERENCES

1 Harold Halt, in *The Schoolhouse in the City*, edited by Alvin Toffler; Frederick A. Praeger, New York, 1968.

2 Jonathan Kozol, *Savage Inequalities* (sub-titled *Children in America's Schools*); Crown Publishers, New York, 1991.

3 Senator Bill Bradley, speech given in the US Senate on 26 March 1992; published in adapted form as 'The Real Lessons of LA', *Harper's Magazine*, New York, July 1992.

4 Ted Kimbrough, quoted in 'Schools in Ruins'; reprint of a series of articles on educational facilities appearing in *Chicago Sun-Times*, 14-18 April 1991.

5 Simon Jenkins, 'London's Forthcoming Boom'; the third (annual) London Weekend Television London Lecture, delivered at the London School of Economics, 25 November 1992.

6 Joel Garreau, *Edge City* (sub-titled *Life on the New Frontier*), published by Doubleday, New York, in 1991, examines the phenomenon of new ex-urban communities and suburban commercial centres in the United States.

7 OECD, *From Megalopolis to City: New Roles for Urban Policies*; a report based on documents for the International Conference on the Economic, Social and Environmental Problems of Cities, 18-20 November 1992, organised by the OECD's Local Initiatives for Employment Creation (ILE) programme, and published as No.11 in the *Innovation & Employment* series, OECD, Paris, April 1993.

8 Richard Weinstein, quoted by Seth Mydans, 'Black and Hispanic Groups Battle Over Schools Post in Los Angeles'; *New York Times*, 5 October 1992.

9 Mike Coombes, Simon Raybould and Cecilia Wong, *Developing Indicators to Assess the Potential for Urban Regeneration*, report of the Inner Cities Directorate of the Department of the Environment; Her Majesty's Stationery Office, London, 1992.

10 Richard Weston, *Schools of Thought* (sub-titled *Hampshire Architecture 1974-1991*); Hampshire County Council, Winchester, England, 1991.

11 Richard Hobbs, in *Schoolhouse in the Red: A Guidebook for Cutting Our Losses*; American Association of School Administrators, Arlington, Virginia, 1992.

12 OECD/PEB, *Providing for Future Change: Adaptability and Flexibility*; OECD, Paris, 1976.

13 Roger Clynes, *Adaptability and Flexibility in Educational Facilities;* OECD, Paris, 1990.

14 Douglas Hibbins, conversation with author, October 1990.

15 *Guidance on Estate Management*; The Further Education Funding Council, Coventry, England, 1993.

16 Michel Noir, quoted by Christiane Nicolas, presentation at OECD/PEB seminar on urban schools, Baltimore, June 1992.

17 Arthur G. Wirth, *Education and Work for the Year 2000: Choices We Face*; Jossey-Bass, San Francisco, 1992.

18 'Building Condition and Student Achievement', in *PEB Exchange* No. 21, OECD, Paris, February 1994. Also: Maureen Berner, 'Building Conditions, Parental Involvement and Student Achievement in the District of Columbia Public School System', in *Urban Education* Vol. 28, No. 1; Sage Publications, Thousand Oaks, California, 1993.

19 Department for Education, Architects and Buildings Branch, *Further Education and Sixth Form Colleges: Development Strategies for Accommodation*; Department for Education, London, 1992.

20 Kenneth Baker, *The Turbulent Years*; Faber and Faber, London, 1993.

21 Department for Education, 'Survey of Information Technology in Schools'; *Statistical Bulletin 6/93*, Department for Education, London, 1993.

22 Norman Willis, *New Technology and Its Impact on Educational Buildings*; OECD, Paris, 1992.

23 Milton Goldberg, quoted by Meg Sommerfeld, 'Time and Space', in *From Risk to Renewal* by the editors of *Education Week*; Editorial Projects in Education, Washington DC, 1993.

24 Teun van Wijk, presentation at OECD/PEB seminar on urban schools, Baltimore, June 1992.

25 *From Risk to Renewal*, op. cit., and various local evaluations in the USA.

26 Julia Hagedorn, *The Longer School Day and Five Term Year in City Technology Colleges: Some Initial Observations*; City Technology Colleges Trust, London, 1992. Also see: *Electronic Registration*, a research and development paper published by the same organisation.

27 Brian Knight, *Managing School Time*; Longman, London, 1989.

28 Richard Lynn, *Educational Achievement in Japan: Lessons for the West*; Macmillan, London, 1988.

29 Her Majesty's Inspectors, *Taught Time: An Interim Report*; Office for Standards in Education, London, 1994.

30 Michael Rutter, Barbara Maughan, Peter Mortimore and Janet Ouston, *Fifteen Thousand Hours* (sub-titled: *Secondary Schools and Their Effects on Children*); Open Books, London, 1979.

31   Wendy Titman, *Special Places: Special People*; Learning Through Landscapes, Winchester, England, 1994.

32   Michael Field, quoted by Mike Duckenfield, 'The College Campus of the Future', in *PEB Exchange* No. 18; OECD, Paris, February 1993.

33   John Bolton, quoted by Mike Duckenfield, 'The College Campus of the Future', op. cit.

34   OECD, *High Quality Education and Training for All*; analytical report prepared for meeting of education ministers of member countries, in Paris,13-14 November 1990, and subsequently published with other material as report with same title, OECD, Paris, 1992.

35   Industrial R&D Advisory Committee of the Commission of the European Communities (IRDAC), *Opinion on Skill Shortages in Europe*; Commission of the European Communities, Brussels, 1990.

36   Further Education Unit, *Open College Networks: Participation and Progression*; Further Education Unit, London, 1993.

37   Office for Standards in Education, *Access and Achievement in Urban Education*; Her Majesty's Stationery Office, London, 1993. (The seven cities and towns involved in this survey were Bristol, Derby, Kingston-upon-Hull, London, Manchester, Slough and Tilbury/Thurrock.)

38   Handsworth College features in Harminder Aujla, William Baidoe-Ansah, Subash Ranjani and Mohammed Aslam Sharriff, *Educational Guidance: New Responses for Inner Cities* by ; Further Education Unit, London, 1989.

39   Julia Hagedorn, 'A New Work Environment for Teachers', in *Replan Review* No.6; Department of Education and Science, London, 1991.

40   Graeme Draper and John Jackson, *Training On The Move*; Department of Education and Science, London, 1988.

41   *Quality Education and Training for the Adult Unemployed*, published by the Further Education Unit, London, in 1992, is a manual for planners and managers in colleges developed from the experience of the UK government's REPLAN programme, which sought to promote good practice in adult learning (particularly for the unemployed) during the 1980s. Also: *Access in Action: Breaking Down the Barriers*, published by the Unit in 1989.

42   Department for Education, *Further Education and Sixth Form Colleges: Development Strategies for Accommodation*, op. cit.

43   George Eliot, *The Mill on The Floss*; first published 1860, numerous editions.

44   Ray Marshall and Marc Tucker, *Thinking for a Living* (sub-titled *Education and the Wealth of Nations*); Basic Books, New York, 1992.

45 Robin Hambleton, *Urban Government in the 1990s* (sub-titled *Lessons from the USA*); School for Advanced Urban Studies, University of Bristol, England, 1990.

46 Christopher Jencks, *Rethinking Social Policy* (sub-titled *Race, Poverty and the Underclass*); Harvard University Press, Cambridge, Massachusetts, 1992.

47 Office for Standards in Education, *The Technology Schools Initiative 1992-1993*; Her Majesty's Stationery Office, London, 1994.

48 Mike Duckenfield, *Vocational Education and Training in Europe*, a four-country study in four employment sectors; Further Education Unit, London, 1992.

49 CERTA is described in Donald Hirsch, *Schools and Business: A New Partnership*; OECD, Paris, 1992.

50 Business Roundtable, *Participation Guide: A Primer for Business on Education*; Business Roundtable, New York, 1991.

51 Peter F. Drucker, *Innovation and Entrepreneurship*; Harper & Row, New York, 1985.

52 John Mayfield and Kelvin Trimper, 'Golden Grove: A Secondary Education Complex in South Australia', No. 5 in the *Long-Term Perspectives* series; OECD, Paris, 1989.

53 Theodore R. Sizer, quoted in *From Risk to Renewal*, op. cit.

54 Anne Ratzki interviewed in American Educator (magazine) and quoted by George Leonard, 'The End of School'; *The Atlantic Monthly*, Boston, Massachusetts, May 1992.

55 Seymour Fliegel with James MacGuire, *Miracle in East Harlem* (sub-titled *The Fight for Choice in Public Education*); Times Books, New York, 1993.

56 Joseph A. Fernandez (with John Underwood), *Tales Out of School*; Little, Brown and Company, Boston, 1993.

57 The Council of the Great City Schools, *National Urban Education Goals: Baseline Indicators, 1990-91*; The Council of the Great City Schools, Washington DC, 1992.

58 James P. Comer, quoted by Michele Ingrassia, 'The World Without Fathers'; *Newsweek*, 30 August 1993.

59 National Alliance of Business, *A Blueprint for Business on Restructuring Education*; National Alliance of Business, Washington DC, 1989.

60 US Census Bureau, *Family Disruption and Economic Hardship: The Short-Run Picture for Children*; US Government Printing Office, Washington DC, 1991.

61   US Census Bureau, *Children's Well-Being: An International Comparison*;
     US Government Printing Office, Washington DC, 1990.

62   Findings of the National Survey on Children, a longitudinal study
     begun in 1976, are referred to by Barbara Dafoe Whitehead, 'Dan
     Quayle Was Right'; *The Atlantic Monthly*, Boston, Massachusetts,
     April 1993.

63   Joyce Epstein, quoted in article by Deborah L. Cohen; *Education
     Week*, Washington DC, 17 June 1992.

64   Sir Christopher Ball, *Start Right: The Importance of Early Learning*;
     Royal Society for the encouragement of Arts, Manufactures and
     Commerce (RSA), London, 1994.

65   Office for Standards in Education, *Access and Achievement in Urban
     Education*, op. cit.

66   Dervla Murphy, *Tales from Two Cities*; John Murray (Publishers) Ltd.,
     London, 1987.

67   *Access and Achievement in Urban Education*, op. cit.

68   Lawrence J. Schweinhart and David P. Weikart, *A Summary of Significant
     Benefits: The High/Scope Perry Pre-School Study Through Age 27*;
     High/Scope Research Institute, Ypsilanti, Michigan, 1993.

69   For more examples, see *PEB Exchange* No. 20; OECD, Paris, October
     1993. Also, a fuller report by the OECD Programme on Educational
     Building on out-of-hours schemes is in preparation.

70   Kids' Clubs Network, *Report of Survey of Schools' Out-of-School Care
     Provision*; Kids' Clubs Network, London, 1990.

71   US Education Department, *National Study of Before and After School
     Programs*; US Education Department, Office of Policy and Planning,
     Washington DC, 1993.

72   Ahmed Jasim, quoted by Eugene Robinson, 'Sweden's Ambivalent
     Embrace'; *Washington Post* (weekly edition), 9-15 August 1993.

73   Chenjerai Hove, in *Common Cause* (magazine), Chard, Somerset,
     England, July-September 1993 edition.

74   Theo Veld, 'Urban Educational Issues in The Netherlands', in *World
     Yearbook of Education 1992: Urban Education*, edited by David Coulby,
     Crispin Jones and Duncan Harris; Kogan Page, London, 1992.

75   Committee of Inquiry into the Education of Children from Ethnic
     Minority Groups, *West Indian Children in Our Schools* (interim report)
     and *Education For All* (final report); Her Majesty's Stationery Office,
     London, 1981 and 1985, respectively.

76 House of Commons Home Affairs Committee, *Chinese Community in Britain* (three volumes); Her Majesty's Stationery Office, London, 1985.

77 Claude M. Steele, 'Race and the Schooling of Black Americans'; *The Atlantic Monthly*, Boston, Massachusetts, April 1992.

78 Molefi Kete Asante, quoted by Jerry Adler et. al., 'African Dreams'; *Newsweek*, 23 September 1991.

79 Mary Jordan, 'On Track Toward Two-Tier Schools'; *Washington Post* (national weekly edition), 31 May - 6 June 1993.

80 Shelby Steele, *The Content of Our Character* (sub-titled *A New Vision of Race in America*); St Martin's Press, New York, 1990.

81 Kozol, op. cit.

82 Richard Riley, quoted in *Atlanta Constitution*, 13 June 1993.

83 Crime Concern, *Memorandum of Evidence to Inquiry into Juvenile Crime of the Home Affairs Committee*, House of Commons, London, submitted 12 January 1993.

84 National Commission on Children, *Beyond Rhetoric* (sub-titled *A New American Agenda for Children and Families*), final report of commission chaired by Senator John D. ("Jay") Rockefeller IV; US Government Printing Office, Washington DC, 1991.

85 Hiroshi Kimura, Haruo Sato and Asahiro Arai, 'Tokyo: Urbanization and Education', in *World Yearbook of Education 1992: Urban Education*, edited by David Coulby, Crispin Jones and Duncan Harris; Kogan Page, London, 1992.

86 Roger Graef, *Living Dangerously, Young Offenders in Their Own Words*; HarperCollins, London, 1992.

87. Inspector Dick Groves, Scotland Yard Crime Prevention Unit, quoted by Duncan Campbell; *The Guardian*, London, 12 December 1992.

88 Victor Herbert, quoted by Karl Zinsmeister, 'Growing Up Scared'; *The Atlantic Monthly*, Boston, Massachusetts, June 1990.

89 Zinsmeister, op. cit.

90 Findings of the first annual survey are reported by Douglas Lederman, 'Colleges Report 7 500 Violent Crimes on Their Campuses in First Annual Statements Required under Federal Law'; *The Chronicle of Higher Education*, Washington DC, 20 January 1993.

91 Timothy D. Crowe, quoted in 'Crime Draws Some of the Lines in Blueprints for Schools'; *New York Times*, 6 March 1991. Also: the same author, 'Designing Safer Schools'; *School Safety*, Autumn 1990 issue.

92 Department of Education and Science, 'Closed Circuit TV Surveillance Systems in Educational Buildings'; *Building Bulletin 75*, Department of Education and Science, Her Majesty's Stationery Office, London, 1991.

93 Gerald Haigh, *Using Technology to Combat Truancy*; The City Technology Colleges Trust, London, 1993.

94 Department of Education and Science, 'Crime Prevention in Schools – Practical Guidance'; *Building Bulletin 67*, Department of Education and Science, Her Majesty's Stationery Office, London, 1987.

95 David Hart, quoted by James Meikle, 'Schools Fight £53m a year Crime Bill'; *The Guardian*, London, 27 January 1993.

96 US General Accounting Office, *Drugs Education: School-based Programs Seen as Useful but Impact Unknown*, report to the chairman of the Senate Committee on Governmental Affairs; US Government Printing Office, Washington DC, 1990.

97 Fred. M. Hechinger, *Fateful Choices* (sub-titled *Healthy Youth for the 21st Century*); Carnegie Corporation of New York/ Carnegie Council on Adolescent Development, New York, 1992.

98 Brainard Braimah is reported in *Seen IT in the UK*, a report of visits to schemes in Britain making an innovative use of information technology carried out during the autumn of 1993; National Council for Educational Technology, Coventry, England, 1994. The school is also reported in Elizabeth Crowther-Hunt and Lucy Billingshurst, *Inner Cities, Inner Strengths*; Industrial Society Press, London, 1990.

99 Carnegie Corporation, *A Matter of Time*, report of the Task Force on Youth Development and Community Programs; Carnegie Corporation of New York/ Carnegie Council on Adolescent Development, New York, 1992.

100 Léon Bing, *Do or Die*; HarperCollins, New York, 1991.

101 *Access and Achievement in Urban Education*, op. cit.

102 John Kenneth Galbraith, *The Culture of Contentment*; Houghton Mifflin Company, New York, 1992.

103 Lord Scarman, *The Brixton Disorders*; Her Majesty's Stationery Office, London, 1981.

104 Deyan Sudjic, *The 100 Mile City*; André Deutsch, London, 1992.

105 Report of the National Commission on Excellence in Schools, *A Nation at Risk*; Department of Education, Washington DC, 1983. Also *Competence and Competition*, report by the National Economic Development Office; Manpower Services Commission, Sheffield, England, 1984. The quote is from the follow-up report, *A Challenge to Complacency*, published by the Manpower Services Commission in 1985.

106 *Learning to Succeed*, report of the National Commission on Education; Heinemann, London, 1993.

107 Joe Schneider, 'Can the Schoolhouse Handle Systemic Reform?'; *Education Week*, Washington DC, 9 June 1993.

108 Quoted by Schneider, op. cit.

109 David Osborne and Ted Gaebler, *Reinventing Government* (sub-titled *How the Entrepreneurial Spirit is Transforming the Public Sector*); Allison-Wesley, Reading, Massachusetts, 1992.

110 Changes in the role and responsibilities of government, being implemented in many countries, are discussed in Thierry Malan, *Decentralisation and Educational Building Management: The Impact of Recent Reforms*; OECD, Paris, 1992.

111 For a full discussion of recent trends, see Donald Hirsch, *Schools and Business: A New Partnership*; OECD, Paris, 1992.

112 Robin Squire, speech to conference of the Federation of Civil Engineering Contractors, Queen Elizabeth II Conference Centre, London, 25 October 1993.

113 Peter Schmidt, 'Management Firm Finds Schools a Tough Sell'; Education Week, Washington DC, 14 October 1992. Also, unsigned, 'Public Schools Better in Hands of Profit-Makers?'; *Atlanta Constitution*, 27 June 1993.

114 John E. C. MacBeath, *Home From School – Its Current Relevance*; Jordanhill College of Education, Glasgow, Scotland, 1989.

115 Drucker, op. cit.

116 Mike Duckenfield, 'A Question of Quality', in *PEB Exchange* No. 17, OECD, Paris, October 1992.

117 David Drew, John Gray and Nicholas Sime, *Against the Odds: The Education and Labour Market Experiences of Black Young People*, report of the England and Wales Youth Cohort Study; Employment Department, Sheffield, England, 1992.

118 Jane Jacobs, *The Death and Life of Great American Cities*; Random House, New York, 1961.

119 Jencks, op. cit.

120 Scarman, op. cit.

121 David Robins, *Tarnished Vision* (sub-titled *Crime and Conflict in the Inner City*); Oxford University Press, London, 1992.

122 Ted Kolderie, 'Education That Works: The Right Role for Business'; *Harvard Business Review*, Cambridge, Massachusetts, September/ October 1987.

123   Chris Barnham, 'Inner City Schools That Work: School Improvement in American Cities', in *Better Cities for Better Education; Better Education for Better Cities* by Chris Barnham and Will Wesson; *Education and Training*, vol. 35, no. 6, MCB University Press, Bradford, England, 1993.

124   Her Majesty's Inspectorate, *The Implementation of Local Management of Schools*; Her Majesty's Stationery Office, London, 1992. Also John E. Chubb and Terry M. Moe, *A Lesson in School Reform from Great Britain*; The Brookings Institution, Washington DC, 1992.

125   *Access and Achievement in Urban Education*, op. cit.

126   Kozol, op. cit.

127   John Coons, *Private Wealth and Public Education*; Harvard University Press, Cambridge, Massachusetts, 1970.

128   David Rusk, *Cities Without Suburbs*; Johns Hopkins University Press, Baltimore, 1993.

INTRODUCTION
TO THE CASE STUDIES

The following case studies provide extended descriptions of initiatives involving schools in eight countries. Their locations include major cities such as Athens, New York and Berlin, as well as smaller and less well-known urban communities – Haarlem in the Netherlands and the English railway town of Crewe.

Although the case studies have been provided with headings these can offer no more than a partial advertisement of their content, as each study illustrates more than a single issue or theme. For example, the Victoria Centre in Crewe could just as appropriately have been presented as a study in the community use of schools (its full title is the Victoria Community Centre and High School). To help overcome this, a short list of keywords has been given with each case study.

The studies fall into three groups:

1:   the contribution of education to urban regeneration and physical renewal – a city-wide initiative involving a new suburb (*Adelaide*), a docklands redevelopment (*Gothenburg*), and renovation of inner city districts (*Crewe and Berlin*);

2:   responses by education to developments in society – the need for a technologically sophisticated workforce (*United Kingdom*), social integration (*Greece*), and a reduction in crime (*Haarlem*); and

3:   needs concerning school buildings – city-wide renovation (*Lyon*), better maintenance (*United States*), and new designs for tomorrow's schools (*Edinburgh*).

The case studies are based on material prepared for, or presented at, the OECD/PEB seminar on urban schools, held in Baltimore, in June 1992. Each was updated, where appropriate, to take into account further developments to the spring of 1994, and gives details of relevant publications and contacts. Telephone and fax numbers should be prefaced by international and country codes.

REGENERATION IN A CITY-WIDE CONTEXT

Suburban growth can impact negatively on older neighbourhoods. In particular, it may hasten the loss of jobs (and tax revenues) and divert resources away from already depressed areas. Often it occurs oblivious to the needs of the city as a whole, and it may result in widening disparities between education provision in new and established areas.

The Multi Function Polis project is intended to give Adelaide, and Australia, a valuable niche in emerging markets in technology, the environment and education. It stresses social and environmental aspects in urban redevelopment and includes major new physical infrastructure. The centrepiece is a new suburb whose planning and development is being integrated with the renewal needs of an adjacent district.

The Multi Function Polis and Adelaide

Adelaide is a coastal city of one million people an hour's flight west of its considerably larger neighbours, Melbourne and Sydney. It is the capital of South Australia, a vast territory with more acres than Scandinavia or the three Pacific coast states of the USA combined. One in four South Australians was born overseas, with recent immigration mainly from Asia and the South Pacific. The city's economy has been heavily reliant on manufacturing, notably cars and household appliances, but these industries are declining.

The Multi Function Polis (MFP) is a federally-supported demonstration project aimed at "transforming a typical 20th century city into a model of a 21st century city", and Adelaide was chosen as its site in 1990. If successful, the project will strengthen Australia competitively, especially in the Pacific Rim, through the development of knowledge-based enterprise, in particular that based on information technology and telecommunications, environmental management, and the provision of education.

Central to the project is the development of 3 500 hectares (13.5 sq. mls.) of partially degraded estuarine land about 20 minutes' drive from the city's central business district. This will become a new suburb, projected to house up to 100 000 people by the end of the first decade of the next century. Its design incorporates a mosaic of urban villages, separated by parks, lakes and other natural features (the area includes a substantial mangrove forest), and connected to each other and the rest of the city by state-of-the-art communication and transport systems. Thus, the development stresses city living and urban consolidation rather than sprawl (the site is not peripheral

Downtown Adelaide

The development area with the existing city in the distance

in the usual sense); closeness to the environment; and a human scale characterised by diversity and participation by residents.

The suburb and existing neighbourhoods

The MFP development is a city-wide initiative which focuses on a local development. Its objectives include positioning Adelaide in global markets and using infrastructure development to create a 'systems city'. It also intended that the renewal of rundown neighbourhoods should be an integral part, rather than a by-product, of the new suburban development. "For the new town to be judged a success," says the MFP project's John Mayfield, "the older depressed suburbs adjacent to it must be revitalised in the process."

Close to the new suburb is The Parks. Ironically, it was itself the site of a previous major community development project, featuring large-scale buildings and including theatres, a gymnasium and library. About 50 000 people live in the area, which has poorer health, higher unemployment, and a greater incidence of vandalism and drug abuse than the rest of the city.

The intention to integrate the MFP into the rest of Adelaide, and to ensure that the city as a whole benefits from the new investment, has a number of implications.

● Whenever the MFP project is described, discussed or displayed, the renewal aspects have to be given as much prominence as the new villages.

● Financial and cost-benefit calculations have to take account of impacts on all areas.

● Design of the villages is preceded by urban renewal assessments which set targets to be met by designers, developers and future managers, and some of these targets are described in terms of what must occur in areas adjacent to the new suburb.

The effects of this approach are considerable.

● Unit costs alter as the population of the existing area is brought into the calculations, and funds which would have been allocated for this area can be brought into the equation, as can the existing building stock.

● The proximity and special features of the new development should result in capital appreciation in the existing area (which will also be increased through direct renewal programmes), and capture of these betterments may provide an important source of funds for the project.

● It is possible to rationalise various special programmes, often separately funded and operating from their own premises, for the benefit of the project as a whole.

● Some of the benefits of special assistance for new urban development projects, including infrastructure priorities, tax incentives and government funding, can be applied to the existing areas.

Implications for education

A similar approach has been applied to the educational infrastructure. Thus, when a new school is planned, the design and operation of that school must set out to make a positive contribution to existing, nearby schools.

Hitherto, the challenge in designing a new school has been seen as the creation of a better building than the last. Past mistakes are corrected, and advances in educational technology, construction methods and design are incorporated. This continued, and worthwhile, pursuit of excellence means that each new school tends to set a higher benchmark, thus making existing schools more out-of-date and emphasising the contrast between the worst and the newest.

Instead of directing resources exclusively into the creation of 21st century schools in the new suburb, a proportion of new programmes and specialist facilities will be located in existing schools in other neighbourhoods. This is expected to increase the interdependence of schools, so that the new has to rely on the old, and existing schools will become part of a network which includes the new MFP schools.

Those planning the MFP also see advantages in an integrated approach in terms of efficiency – through eliminating unnecessary duplication, rationalising educational services, and reconfiguring existing schools. The latter could involve the creation of joint ventures between public and parochial (or other) schools, whereby they share specialist facilities on a common campus. (An example of this, in the Adelaide suburb of Golden Grove, is the subject of an OECD/PEB report – see footnote.)

New and renovated schools

MFP planners argue that changes in learning needs and methods, as well as in other areas, mean that educational buildings in both the new suburb and adjacent neighbourhoods should exhibit a number of characteristics, including:

● much greater environmental responsibility, especially in respect of energy and water usage, landscaping including the planting of trees, and recycling and improved waste management;

● enhanced opportunities for interpersonal and group interaction between learners, and between teacher and learner;

● serving as community centres in which people of all ages are likely to be involved, and operating on a 24-hour basis;

● a human and domestic, rather than factory, form and scale; and

● acting as communications centres, providing access to computer technology and high-tech information sources.

Overall, the impact of the MFP project on educational buildings is expected to result in:

● collaboration on a range of facilities issues between the new and old urban areas;

● reconfiguration of existing services and their building components;

● the installation of new information technology to distribute educational services to new and old areas;

● new and upgraded buildings which will be less of a contrast with surrounding urban form;

● buildings which by their design, ownership and operation are themselves renewable; and

● funding, management and ownership arrangements which bring into operation new partnerships between different government agencies, business, and the local community.

Adelaide features as one of seven cities in the OECD study *The Learning City* (see the case study on Lindholmen). 'Golden Grove: A Secondary Education Complex in South Australia', was published as No.5 in the *Long-Term Perspectives* series, by OECD/PEB, in 1989 (see under the Victoria Centre for address). Material about the MFP is available from: John Mayfield, MFP-Australia, Level 12, Terrace Towers, 178 North Terrace, Adelaide, South Australia, 5001 Australia (Tel: +8 226 2100; Fax: +8 226 3665).

PHYSICAL RENEWAL AND AN 'ENTERPRISE CAMPUS'

Many cities have large derelict sites, made redundant by the failure of their ports and the relocation of dock-related industry. Similar, if smaller, sites have also become available, due to the closure of large manufacturing plants and the sale of former railway stations and marshalling yards. From the 1980s, government has developed a variety of plans to revive these areas.

Though close to city centres, the sites and their adjacent neighbourhoods have often become isolated from the flow of urban life – a situation made worse by social deprivation and high unemployment. In Gothenburg, a deliberate attempt is being made to foster the symbiotic links between industrial training, research and production, which are characteristic of cities and essential to innovation.

VOCATIONAL EDUCATION/ TRAINING

HIGHER EDUCATION

LIFELONG LEARNING

SCHOOL/WORK INTERFACES

PLANNING PARTNERSHIP

SHARED USED

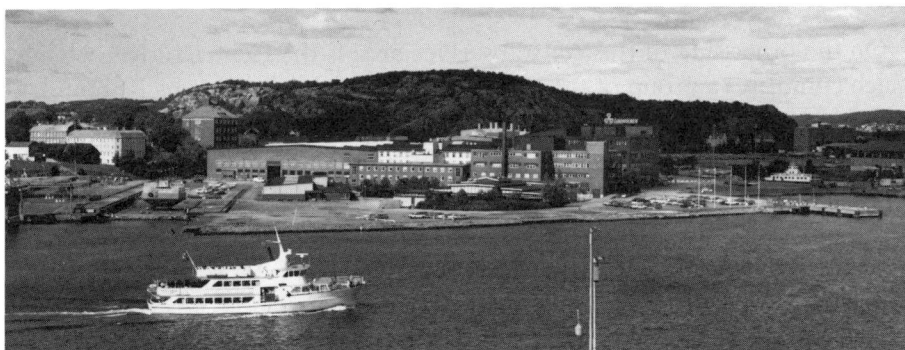

The Centre of Knowledge at Lindholmen, in Gothenburg

With just over 400 000 residents, Gothenburg is Sweden's second city. On the west (rather than Baltic) coast it provided ready access to the world's seaways and, for 130 years, was home to a thriving shipping industry. But with the demise of the port in the mid-1970s, the dock area, which is located on the opposite bank of the Göta River to the city centre, stood silent for a decade.

In the mid-1980s the Lindholmen Development Corporation was created to refurbish and restore the docklands as an integrated zone featuring educational and research facilities, light industrial and service companies, and new homes.

The Centre of Knowledge at Lindholmen is a multi-purpose education, training and research complex integrating provision for upper secondary school students (aged 16-19) and adult and higher education. It occupies slightly more than half of the development zone (which comprises 240 000 square metres, or nearly 60 acres), with the remainder fairly evenly divided between business facilities and 465 residential apartments.

While most of the buildings are new, a core of former dock buildings has been retained. The layout of the zone is as follows:

● One side comprises a long, oblong area, almost half of which forms a pier into the river. Half of the length of this area will be residential – with apartments for students, local workers and the elderly – and the other is to be occupied by six new, and one existing, commercial and industrial buildings.

● Adjacent to the pier a landscaped area will house two facilities offering services to all who live, study and work at Lindholmen. At one end, next to the river ferry terminus, is a community centre with a restaurant, library and auditorium; at the other, next to a municipal tram stop, there is a hotel, shopping and conference centre.

● On the other side of this central service area is the Centre of Knowledge, which comprises a group of more than a dozen buildings, of which about half have been remodelled and refurbished and the rest are newly-built.

● Surrounding the centre on its other sides are additional buildings – all but one new – in which are housed further workshops and offices, and the riverfront.

The concept behind the Centre of Knowledge involves the close integration of:

● upper secondary school technical and vocational courses (for 16-19 year-olds);

● municipal adult education;

● national and regional training programmes for the unemployed;

● corporate industrial training;

● higher education and research; and

● industrial production.

To achieve this, the City of Gothenburg (which owns the docklands) has brought together a partnership including the city's board of education, one of Gothenburg's two universities (Chalmers University of Technology), the county employment and training board, the national agency for occupational training, adult education colleges and associations, and individual companies. Its overall aim is "to implement basic and advanced training in areas of importance to the Gothenburg region".

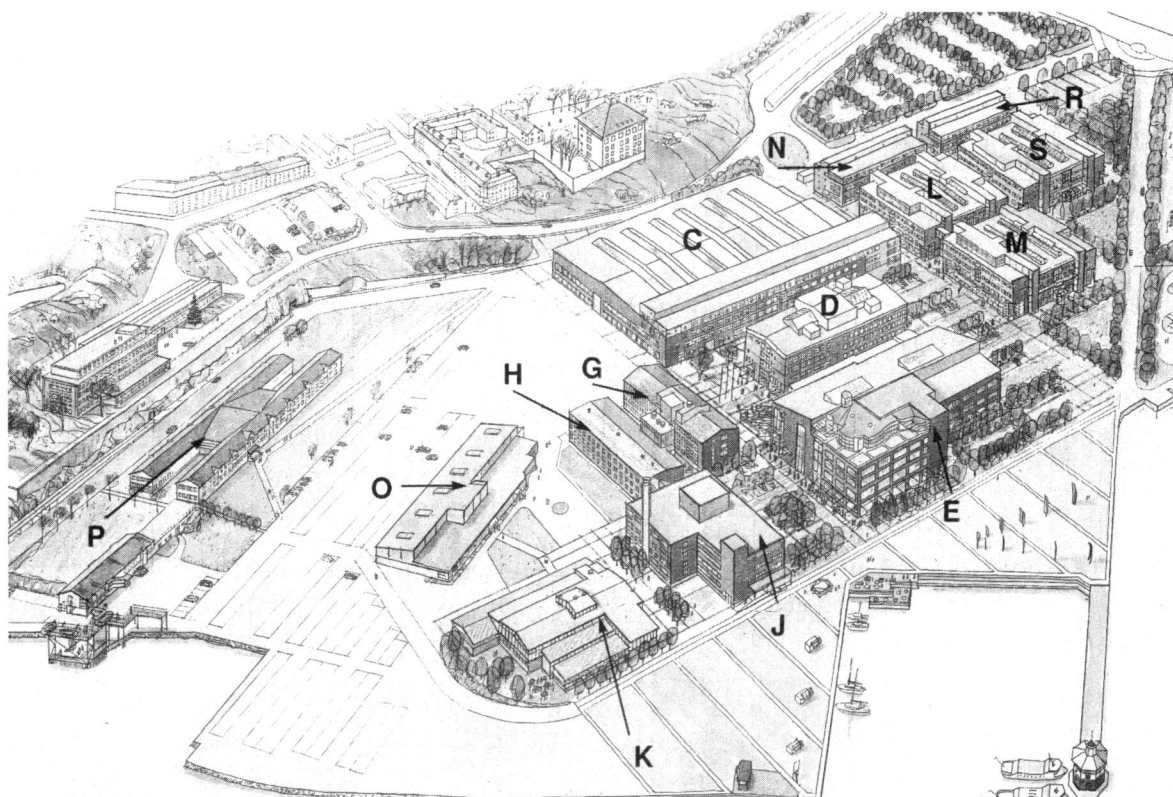

*A plan of the Centre of Knowledge as it is expected to be in 1995 Buildings include, among others (right to left): **P** - classrooms for core subjects taken during the first year of the upper secondary curriculum and administrative offices; **O** - specialist facilities used by the neighbourhood upper secondary school and the district adult education service (also **G** and **H**, which also includes the offices of the company that manages the Lindholmen development area; and **J**, which is a centre for studies in the natural sciences); **K** - a cafeteria restaurant; **D** - a former marine engineering factory converted to house a catering school linked to two restaurants and a shop where students sell their bakery products; **L** and **M** - new buildings to be occupied by Chalmers University; and **N, R** and **S** - also newly-built, these will comprise the Building and Construction Centre shared by Chalmers and others.*

*Page 103: Lindholmen as it was in 1992. The long building behind the ferry (**C** on the plan) is a former shipyard factory converted to provide vocational training courses on which the unemployed, who are subsidised, and fee-paying company employees study together. To the right, the building with the Lindholmen sign on the roof (**E** on the plan) is being remodelled for completion in autumn 1994. It will house a media resources centre and programmes on electrical engineering and energy production, which will cater both for 16-19 year-olds and adults.*

In essence, Lindholmen operates as a kind of science park, comprising a number of 'institutes'. Each covers a different subject area and integrates technical education, industrial training, research and production. Industrial training courses (which are fee-based) and technical upper secondary school courses (which are free) may thus be located adjacently in the same building. Thus, for example, The Centre of Production Technology, which opened in 1986, enables school students to meet daily with course participants from companies such as Volvo and the bearings firm SKF (both of which have their headquarters in Gothenburg).

Commercial space at Lindholmen is only available to firms that will provide qualified training and study practice places for students at the knowledge centre, while the allocation of space within the centre's buildings also characterises partnership: in several, upper secondary school facilities have been created alongside those of either adult and higher education, or both.

The knowledge centre is expected to be fully operational by the mid-1990s, when it will have grown to a community of about 5 000 students, teachers and other personnel. Several 'institutes' have started work, including, in addition to that for production technology, those for the training of professional drivers, and hotel and catering workers, as well as centres for electrical engineering, energy and the environment, materials handling, and shipping.

Recent developments include:

● Introduction of an experimental upper secondary education syllabus, called technical production and service, developed by the city's board of education, Chalmers and the national agency for occupational training, and which will enable 1 120 students in 70 classes (class size of 15 students) to take 'integrated' courses at Lindholmen.

● Removal to Lindholmen of an upper secondary school offering courses for the construction industry, and part of a school offering courses for the catering industry.

● Provision of 28 000 hours of upper secondary level tuition for adults, by the city's adult education service (Komvux), at Lindholmen.

Kunskapscentrum på Lindholmen, a booklet with plans describing the project, was published by Stadsbyggnadskontoret Göteborg (the Gothenburg Office of Buildings), in 1991. Some material in English is also available. Contact Christian Kallerdahl, Utbildningsnämnd, Box 5428, 402 29 Gothenburg, Sweden (Tel: +31 35 30 00; Fax: +31 83 24 52). Lindholmen and Gothenburg feature in *The Learning City*, an OECD study looking at ways in which seven cities are creating lifelong learning cultures. Published in 1993 by Gothenburg Education Committee, it is priced US $20 or equivalent and can be ordered from Christina Gustavsson at the address above.

URBAN RENOVATION AND SCHOOL BUILDING

New and renovated schools can be beneficial additions to the urban landscape both in themselves and by being a part of, or stimulating, wider improvements. The latter typically occurs when social objectives are set for school building schemes, for example as in Berlin, where old schools have been extensively remodelled and retained in inner city districts so that they can serve as social and cultural centres for immigrants and foreign-born residents.

Extending community use to schools is another means by which general infrastructure improvements may be effected, provided education authorities co-ordinate the planning of school building projects with other levels and branches of government, as the creation of the Victoria Centre in Crewe shows.

COMMUNITY USE

CO-ORDINATED PLANNING

NEIGHBOURHOOD SCHOOLS

IMMIGRATION

HOUSING IMPROVEMENT

RECREATION/ YOUTH

The Victoria Centre, Crewe, England

At first glance the county of Cheshire seems mostly rural – a breath of green space between industrial Manchester and Merseyside to the north and the large West Midlands conurbation to the south. In fact, it consists mainly of small and medium-sized towns many of which are industrial in character. These act as focuses for the eight administrative districts (boroughs) into which the county, which is the local education authority and has a population of nearly a million, is divided.

Crewe, one of these towns, was created by a railway company and, for over a 100 years, thrived as an important junction and trans-shipment centre. However, since the 1960s, modernisation and the loss of business to road transport has drastically reduced rail employment, and this decline exposed Crewe as being in something of a time-warp: it had not changed much this century. When county planners broached the idea of the Victoria Centre, it was widely derided. "It won't work in Crewe," they said.

Background

The county was reorganising its secondary schools in line with the national change to 'comprehensive' schools in place of separate academic 'grammar' and general 'secondary modern' schools. A new, unified high school was to be established, but there was insufficient money to build entirely new premises. Moreover, choice of a new green field site would have meant removing the school to the edge of town, away from the neighbourhood it was to serve.

The solution to these constraints was to combine upgrading of an existing school with an incremental programme of separate, smaller new buildings –

107

and to include in each an element of community use, thus enabling the project to draw on additional resources. The project was jointly managed by the county, responsible for education, and the borough, which is responsible for leisure and community services. The end result would be creation of the Victoria Community Centre and High School.

Phases

● Upgrading of Ludford Street School. Built in 1931 as an elementary school and located on a cramped site made worse by the use of no fewer than 27 huts and mobile classrooms, this school was one of the town's least successful. It was transformed into a semi-self-contained lower school for 11-13 year-olds. Parts of the building were also equipped for casual (drop-in) community use, including a mothers' and toddlers' centre, youth club for 9-13 year-olds and activities centre for senior citizens.

● Between the school and the town centre lay an area of 19th century terrace (row) houses which was suffering from dereliction and blight caused by planning indecision. Vacant sites cleared for an aborted retail development were free, and it was decided to build three separate centres, in sequence, as finances permitted. Each centre has space for use by the community.

The first to be built was the single-storey Newdigate Centre, which has teaching facilities for business and technical studies and the humanities. It also contains a music performance studio, central lecture theatre, lounge and coffee bar.

The Oakley building provides space for science and language teaching and sports. A multi-purpose hall has six badminton courts; there is a weight-training room; a gallery which can be used for everything from indoor bowls to wedding receptions; and licensed bars and a cellar for storing beer and wine.

The Meredith building includes a drama studio and workshop; teaching space for English and arts and craft subjects; the school library; a coffee bar and refectory; and facilities for a pre-school play group.

● A school and community sports ground has been created on reclaimed derelict railway land. It includes all-weather sports pitches and a running track to regional competition standards.

Benefits

Created over a three-year period just over a decade ago, the Victoria Centre proved to be an immediate success.

Community use quickly rose to about 300 000 attendances a year, roughly equivalent to four times the town's population. Facilities are open seven days a week, almost throughout the year, and uses not already mentioned

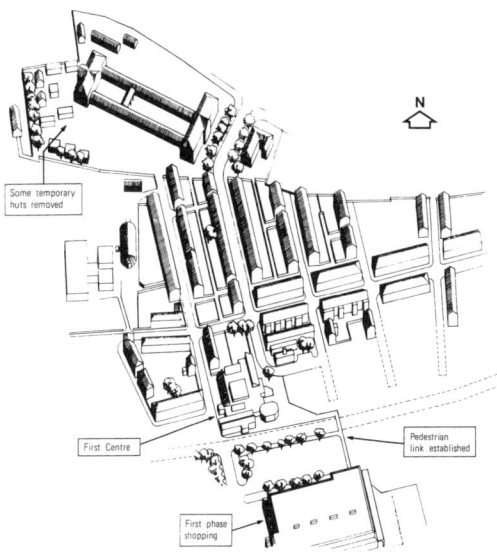

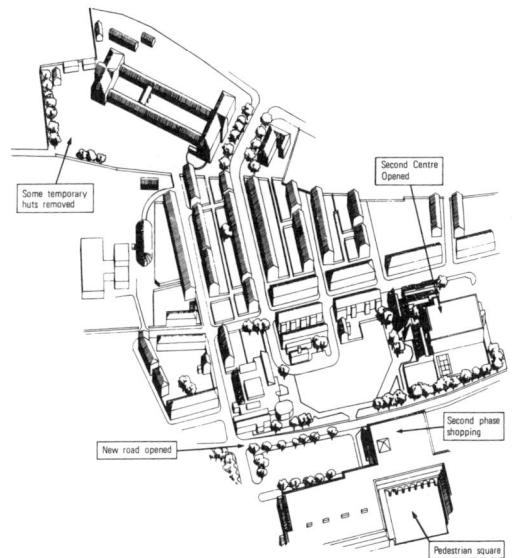

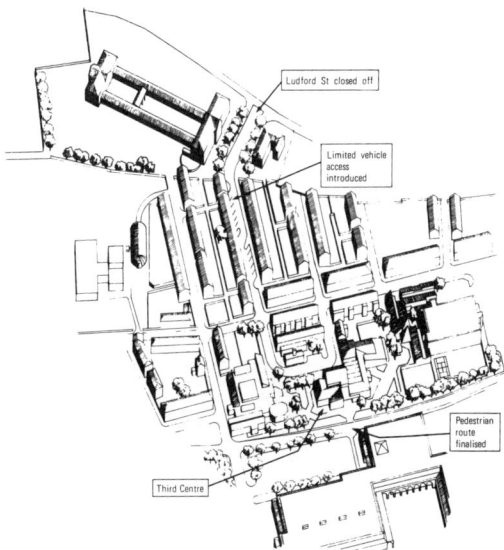

1   First stage of the Crewe development, showing Ludford Street School (north) and the site to be developed (south), with intermediate housing.

2   Second stage, with further removal of temporary huts at Ludford Street, the creation of a new road, the second building of the Victoria Centre, and further retail developments.

3   Third stage, with all temporary buildings removed and the Victoria Centre completed.

include for adult education courses, lettings for meetings by hobby groups and neighbourhood associations, and promotional activities by local government. There has also been increased parental involvement in the school.

Parental demand to enrol their children in the high school has greatly increased (in fact, the school is now the most popular of the town's three high schools). Factors given credit for this include the split site, which allows 11-13 year-olds to be in a transitional environment between primary school and 'young adulthood', and the existence of the mothers and toddlers' centre in the lower school, which has created a social focal point for mothers in the neighbourhood (particularly, it is said, for those new to the area and those living in public housing).

The school's principal says the furbishment of the school for community use – with carpets and attractively furnished social areas – has had a "civilising effect", and movement between the sites acts as a sort of safety valve for teenage energy.

Significantly, the Victoria Centre project has also had several 'knock-on' benefits for the neighbourhood environmentally, including:

● landscaping in conjunction with the creation of a new urban highway (which has enabled the town centre to be pedestrianised);

● housing improvement - the once rundown terraced houses have increased in value and gap sites in the neighbourhood have been developed as homes for rent by non-profit housing associations; and

● influencing decisions on the scale and design of a new shopping centre (whose car park doubles as the centre's car park).

Ludford Street and school three years before redevelopment began

The Nehring School and Adolf Damaschke School, Berlin

Charlottenburg and Kreuzberg are inner city districts of what was West Berlin. They were developed towards the end of the last century, and are characterised by neighbourhoods (or quarters) consisting of blocks of densely built rows of houses and tenements, divided by side streets, between broad boulevards.

The populations of both districts, like those of other rundown parts of the city, include high proportions of immigrants and foreign-born residents whose social integration is regarded as an important task of urban redevelopment. Renovation of old schools provides an opportunity to keep schools in their present location, where they can be developed as a social and cultural focus for the district, and to create modern learning environments while retaining the distinctive appearance of the area.

The Nehring School, Charlottenburg

The school buildings on the Nehringstrasse were constructed in the 1890s and lay in an area earmarked for redevelopment, the objectives of which were to retain residents in the district by "creating a forward-looking inner city housing area" while perpetuating the district's architectural character.

Although the ground area of the schools – the Nehring Elementary School and adjacent Peter Jordan Special School – was small by current standards (it comprises 2.5 hectares or 5.5 acres), it was decided that it would be adequate, provided the existing buildings were retained and a very compact design for the extensions was utilised.

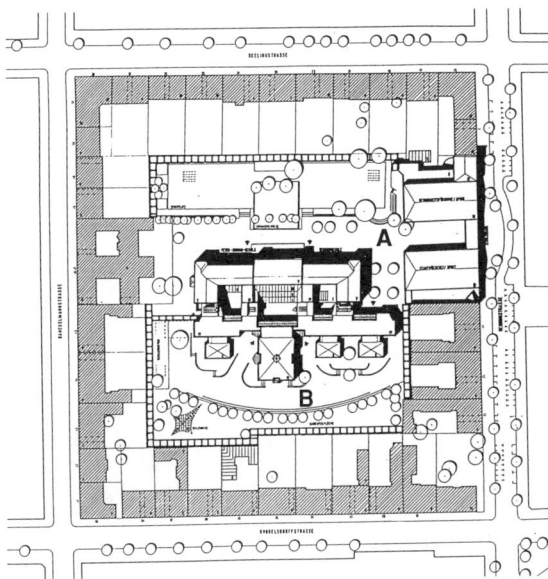

The Nehring School and Peter Jordan Special School share a site within a neighbourhood block. The entrance, where the street has been narrowed, is between a municipal library and a district health centre.

*The view leaving the campus, towards Nehringstrasse (from **A** on the plan)*

*The back of the complex, of which both buildings are part (from **B** on the plan)*

URBAN RENOVATION AND SCHOOL BUILDING

Even before the recent influx of immigrants and refugees into Germany, half the students in the elementary school and one in four in the special school were children of foreign-born parents, and with this in mind a preliminary report on renovation of the schools concluded:

"The location seems ideal for the catchment area, also with regard to the possibility of making [the schools] the district's central point by means of social and recreational facilities. The proposed community facilities are ideally located in the residential area, in a place where a self-contained, single-purpose school site cannot be justified from the town planning viewpoint. Through joint or multi-purpose use of the facilities, more economic utilisation of ground and building areas and savings on staff, materials and maintenance costs are to be expected."

The project comprised a four-storey elementary school (to age 12), a two-storey special school for children with learning difficulties (ages 6-16), a school library, a city library, district health care centre, sports field and running track. The area is entirely enclosed within a street block, that is, surrounded by the backs of houses – except for a landscaped entrance on Nehringstrasse. The new health centre and city library stand on opposite sides of this entrance, the gap between them forming a gateway to the schools.

Adolf Damaschke School, Kreuzberg

The Adolf Damaschke School stands within a triangular block on Skalitzer Strasse and was built in 1886 to accommodate 600 boys and the same number of girls. The building was ill-suited to meet the educational requirements of the late-20th century. Even before unification almost four in five students were foreign-born, and housing in the neighbourhood had been neglected for decades.

Discussion between the education authority, architects and local residents led to the decision to try and make renovation of the school a catalyst for general improvement, particularly of housing. The intention was to run the project as a pilot to test the possibilities of survival for schools in particularly deprived areas, and to help eliminate deprivation in these areas.

The guiding concept was that the school should be seen as part of the neighbourhood and, accordingly, physical changes in the school were accompanied by revisions in the curriculum and teaching.

● The school was no longer to be self-contained. Instead, areas around the buildings were opened up and made part of the neighbourhood. They include sports facilities, a *boule* alley, adventure playground and gardens. By improving the appearance of the area it was hoped to stimulate the renovation of adjacent housing (as occurred in Crewe).

The old building at Adolf Damaschke School, showing two of the added towers

● To save valuable space in the courtyard area, new teaching areas were created by altering and extending the school – notably by inserting a new floor within the roof of the old school. Other alterations included reorganising classroom spaces into clusters, so breaking down the institutional 'feel' of the original building where rooms were rigidly arranged along corridors. The clusters of rooms are supplemented by new spaces for group work which are stacked up as towers on both sides of the building.

● A new building for joint school and community use was made the focal point of the complex. It contains two sports halls, a library, and arts and craft facilities (including baking kilns, and a photo laboratory and dark room).

● To aid social integration, teachers work in teams, each team remaining with the same students as they progress through grades 7-10 (ages 13-16). To ease transition of new entrants to the school, the curriculum for the seventh grade was redesigned to include practical projects which students carry out in the local community. Current enrolment is about 370 students.

The UK Department of Education and Science published *The Victoria Centre, Crewe: School and Community Provision in Urban Renewal*, as *Building Bulletin 59*, in 1981. This is no longer in print, but photocopies of the text may be obtained from the Architects and Buildings Technical Library, Department for Education, Sanctuary Buildings, Great Smith Street, London SW1P 3BT, United Kingdom. Subsequently published, and still available, is *The Victoria Centre, Crewe; An Update*, which appeared as *A&B Paper 8*, in 1985. This is free, from Department for Education Publications, PO Box 2193, London E15 2EU (Tel: +81 533 2000; Fax: +81 533 7700). A comprehensive illustrated article about the Victoria Centre, by Tony Aldous, appeared in the 21 November 1984 issue of *The Architects' Journal*, London. Information about the centre also features in Roger Clynes, *Adaptability and Flexibility in Educational Facilities*, OECD, 1990 (available free from OECD/PEB, 2 rue André-Pascal, 75775 Paris Cedex 16, France; Tel: + 1 45 24 92 60; Fax: + 1 45 24 90 98). Contact: Graham Parker, Architects and Building Division, Department for Education, at the above address (Tel: +71 925 5900; Fax: +71 925 6989).

Nehring School, a preliminary report on renovation, is quoted by Gregor Friedl, in Alice C. Veenendaal and Teun J. van Wijk, *The Role of Educational Building in Urban Renewal;* Informatie & Advies Centrum Schoolaccommodaties, Gouda, Netherlands, 1991. Contact: Gregor Friedl, Zentrallstelle für Normungsfragen und Wirtschaftlichkeit im Bildungswesen (ZNWB), Sekretariat der Ständigen Konferenz der Kultusminister der Länder in der Bundesrepublik Deutschland, Schillstrasse 9-10, 1000 Berlin 30, Germany (Tel: +30 2123 2715; Fax: +30 2123 2570).

The new building for shared school and community use

TECHNOLOGY AND BUSINESS-EDUCATION PARTNERSHIP

Mastery of new ways of doing things, such as using computers and the latest processes involved in making artifacts and products, is important for employment in general, but crucial for industry.

Partnership between business and education can help assure the continuing relevance of vocational and technical areas of the curriculum; assist in work experience and vocational counselling; and help students develop the knowledge and skills associated with enterprise. Also, it can bring business resources – financial, material and human – to public education.

City Technology Colleges in the United Kingdom

In 1986, the UK government announced plans to create a network of city technology colleges (CTCs), which would be a new type of secondary school specifically located in inner city and other urban areas, and whose construction and equipping would be part-financed by corporate sponsorship (typically, companies would sponsor and put their name to individual schools). The first opened in 1988, and by 1992 there were fifteen – involving support from the private sector of $53 million.

A language lab at John Cabot College, Bristol.

In the words of the report setting out its current schools policy and plans, *Choice and Diversity: A New Framework for Schools*, published in July 1992, the UK government established the colleges "in partnership with business, to implement an innovative curriculum with a particular emphasis on technology and science, aided by the widespread use of information technology, and to develop new school management practices".

Background

The decision to create CTCs can be seen as complementary to several other measures taken by the UK government in the last decade. These include major funding for the purchase of computers in schools, a national support programme for the development of educational software, and efforts to recruit more mid-career professionals in business and industry into teaching – especially in the sciences and technology.

Of central importance is the creation and implementation, over eight years to 1997, of a National Curriculum which specifies what must be taught to all five to 16 year-olds in public and publicly-supported private schools. Uniquely, this includes a new subject, technology, to be taught throughout the 11 years of 'compulsory' schooling. The curriculum also specifies a number of competences to be developed across a range of subjects. Included, among others, are information technology skills, enterprise and economic awareness, and practical work experience for 14-16 year-olds.

Governance and funding

Every CTC is established as an independent trust with charitable status. The trust is formed jointly by the government and company sponsors, it owns the college and secures its operational independence through a legally binding funding agreement with (national) government. At least 20 per cent of the capital funding is provided by the sponsoring company. The remainder and running costs are met by the government – the latter at an equivalent average rate to that of similar schools maintained by local authorities. A majority of the governing body of each college is comprised of representatives from local industry and commerce.

CTCs charge no fees. Their students are aged 11-19, of all abilities, and are drawn from a defined urban catchment area (of which their composition should be representative). The colleges develop their own curricular philosophies, but must provide the National Curriculum while giving added emphasis to science and technology: at least 30 per cent and not more than 40 per cent of the study week should be devoted to these subjects.

The central co-ordinating body for the CTCs is the City Technology Colleges Trust, also a registered charity. Initially, the trust helped raise corporate sponsorship and find sites for the colleges (including existing school buildings owned by local authorities). It has since extended its role to the general promotion of 'CTC-style' education, curriculum development and innovation, and the provision of training courses and dissemination of good practice.

Developments

1n 1993, the UK parliament passed legislation to extend further the principles underlying the CTCs, to a network of an initial 100 secondary schools which would have "enhanced technology facilities and a commitment to providing courses with a strong vocational emphasis". Not restricted to urban locations, the scheme would enable a lower, but still significant, level of private sponsorship (with companies supplying four representatives to each school governing body). The first 12 schools to be approved as technology colleges were announced in February 1994.

In addition, schools which meet relevant criteria can apply to the CTC Trust to become affiliates. Sixty-three had been accepted, including one in Milwaukee in the United States, by early 1994.

Characteristics

The Essential Educational Characteristics of a CTC Style School sets out extensive checklists of desired requirements for CTCs, technology colleges, and affiliates. These focus on six principal themes, which should be reflected in arrangements covering the curriculum, staff recruitment and development, organisation and management of the school, the creation and use of facilities, and external relations. The themes are:

● promotion of a scientific and technological culture; and of

● a business and industrial culture;

● the "pervasive and discriminating use of information technology";

● "the new vocationalism" – including work experience, vocational guidance testing, and parity of esteem between academic and vocational specialisations post-16;

● internationalism – including an emphasis on language learning, the development of electronic links with schools in other countries, and staff and student exchanges abroad; and

● openness – including school-business partnerships, "the need for schools to market themselves", and greater emphasis on parental involvement and community use.

New technology

Regarding information technology, the checklists specify the following in terms of equipment.

● IT equipment will be visibly present in adequate depth to serve an enriched curriculum.

● There will be a variety of provision related to specialist functions, e.g. in

Students in a workshop area at Kingshurst CTC, Birmingham.

art, music, design, desk-top publishing, and a distributed networking and E-mail system with access as necessary to student and planning records.

● There will be adequate terminals and printers for students' personal use, in work areas, corridors and library spaces.

● Where specialist equipment is concerned, some, and eventually all, of the following will be used:

an IT language teaching centre;

satellite and remote sensing equipment (for use in languages, science and geography);

a computer-aided design and manufacturing (CAD/CAM) suite, programmable equipment, and design, graphics and 3-D modelling facilities for teaching technology;

interactive video systems, CD-ROM and networked CD-ROM;

a multi-purpose computer system for data logging and analysis, covering class scheduling, the maintenance of student and staff records, and a buildings and equipment inventory; and

a multimedia editing and authoring suite for teachers.

In addition:

● IT should be integrated into all areas of the curriculum and be used daily by students, including in writing and numerical work, and the printing out of homework.

● Students should progressively be taught the scientific and technological principles underlying the use of IT – for example, the nature of central processing units, cabling, operating systems, programming languages, and hardware and software engineering.

● All teachers should be competent in the use of E-mail, keyboarding, word processing, graphics and text handling, desk-top publishing, file management, the use of spreadsheets, applications writing, multimedia, the use of databases, information retrieval from CD-ROM and on-line systems, as well as use of IT in their own subject area.

● As regards planning and administration, CTC-style schools should have:

an advisory group or semi-permanent working party – to develop IT policy and which may oversee major purchases including of generic and specialist software;

a development plan for the progressive implementation and use of IT; and

a systems manager whose job centres on the installation and maintenance of hardware and software, the maintenance of network user areas and appropriate back-up procedures, advice on software, and staff training in generic applications.

Innovation

Apart from their use of new technology, CTCs display new approaches in their organisation and other aspects of their work, as these examples show.

ADT COLLEGE, WANDSWORTH, LONDON

The school is divided into five directorates which provide 'cross-curricular mapping'; rooms are designated by directorate, not subject. The directorates cover science, enterprise and world resources, design and technology, language and humanities, and personal development.

The work day is from 8.30 am to 5 pm and divided into 11 units of time. Each unit (or session) comprises 30 minutes. The purpose is to facilitate curricular flexibility. Thus, technology may be taught for three consecutive units (one and a half hours) whereas languages may be taught in intensive half-hour sessions. There are no bells, but there is a five minute changeover period which allows students to relax and chat. There is also a 20-minute mid-morning break and a 75-minute lunch period which includes time for students to take part in enrichment activities (independent study, sports, arts and science workshops). After lunch, and before the five sessions of the afternoon, there is a 20-minute assembly of the school.

ADT College in Wandsworth, London, involved the total refurbishment of buildings, created for a girls' school in 1954, which had been empty for five years. All the buildings have been over-clad with an aluminium curtain-walling system, using double glazing and reflective glass.

The year is divided into five eight-week terms separated by two-week breaks (four weeks from mid-July to mid-August). Thus, the school provides a 200-day year (10 more than the minimum national requirement) as well as 27.5 class hours a week – a total of 5 500 hours per school year (compared to the average of about 4 450 for secondary schools in England and Wales). This does not include the extra minimum 240 hours a year which students spend within the normal school day on enrichment activities. Students' school-based learning week is thus about 30 per cent longer than in most schools.

Teachers at ADT College are expected to work from 8.30 am to 5 pm, including taking part in enrichment activities. Their duties include personal tutoring, with responsibility for guiding and monitoring students' choice of enrichment and academic options, supervising work experience, and liaising with parents, including attending parents' meetings. In addition, they are expected to spend an extra hour each day preparing lessons for the next day. The working year is 42 weeks, which includes two weeks for professional development.

BROOKE WESTON CTC, CORBY
The work day runs from 8.30 am to at least 4 pm, with many students finishing at 6 pm most evenings. Enrichment activities take place daily between 2.15 pm and 4 pm.

Counselling and guidance is provided daily for all students in small tutorial groups which meet for 15 minutes. Small rooms are provided around the college for individual interviews, seminars and quiet study, as well as the tutorial groups.

Time previously spent in registering students is saved by the use of plastic 'swipe cards', which students use to record their presence. The magnetic cards have photographs for identification purposes and a bar code so that they can also be used to make library loans and 'pay' for food in the school's cashless cafeteria.

The curriculum is planned on an open learning model, with differentiated learning programmes, so that students can pursue basic, intermediate or extended studies according to their relative ability, needs and learning rate.

To facilitate this, resource areas have been created within each teaching block (the college is divided into four curriculum management areas). These are positioned in open spaces around the college and in the library. Students use these areas, unsupervised, as part of timetabled classes. Each area makes extensive use of IT equipment for accessing data for work on study assignments.

Designing and building a CTC

EMMANUEL COLLEGE, TYNESIDE

Part of the exterior of Emmanuel College

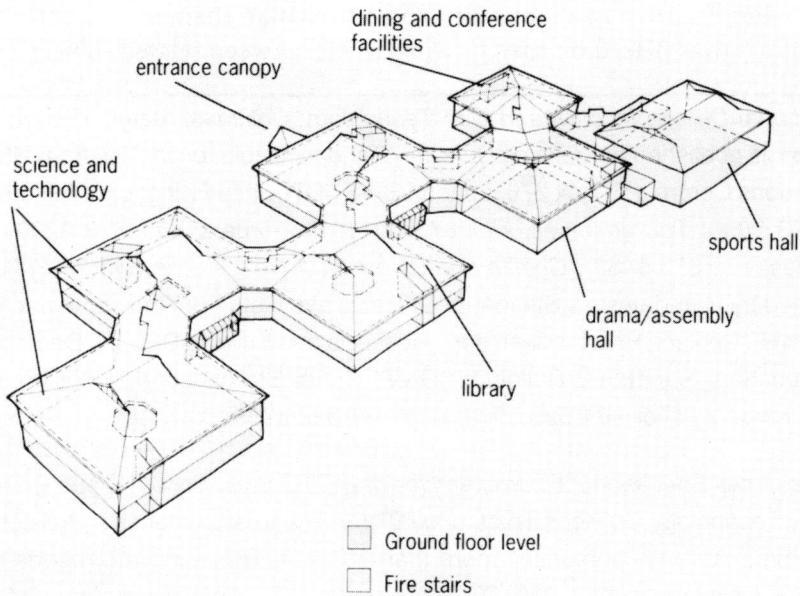

The disposition of space at Emmanuel College, showing the 'necklace' of pavilions – a design style found at several newly-built CTCs.

Emmanuel College is a newly-built school, opened in 1990, situated in Gateshead, a borough of the Tyneside metropolitan area on England's north-east coast. The college has a student capacity of 900 (first-year intake of 150), occupies a site of 2.9 hectares (7.2 acres), has a total gross area of 9 450 square metres (102 000 sq ft) of which 56 per cent is teaching space, and cost $8.6 million to build. The construction was organised so that the college could open and run without hindrance for two months while the last two blocks were finished, enabling the college to be completed in only 15 months.

The design is based on a 'necklace' of repeated pavilions – an approach allowing considerable economy by repetition of detailing, design and construction, particularly as the blocks are all linked in the same way. The five pavilions each have floor areas of 800 square metres (8 600 sq ft), and comprise two storeys. Atria link the pavilions. Four of the pavilions are used for teaching and the other contains an auditorium. In addition, and to one end of the 'necklace', there are two specialist blocks, one for dining and conferencing facilities (including small syndicate rooms), and the other for a sports hall.

A series of teacher rooms and staff offices are located within and between pavilions at each level. This offers good surveillance of the school's courtyards as well as the activities in the pavilions, and good access to the central circulation 'spine'.

The design reflects the school's curricular philosophy which restricts departmentalisation in favour of cross-curricular themes and activities. Emphasis is thus placed on easy, flowing access between related subject areas.

Educational Design Initiatives in City Technology Colleges, featuring six of the colleges, is published as *Building Bulletin 72* and available, price £20, from HMSO Publications Centre, PO Box 276, London SW8 5DT, United Kingdom (Tel. orders: +71 873 9090; Tel. enquiries: +71 873 0011; Fax orders: +71 873 8200; Fax enquiries: +71 873 8463). *Choice and Diversity: A New Framework for Schools*, published by Her Majesty's Stationery Office, is available from the same address, price £8.65. Contact: Beech Williamson, Architects and Building Division, Department for Education, Sanctuary Buildings, Great Smith Street, London SW1P 3BT, United Kingdom (Tel: +71 925 5909; Fax: +71 925 6989).

The Essential Educational Characteristics of a CTC Style School is published by the City Technology Colleges Trust, price £7.50. The trust's extensive publications programme currently comprises more than 40 titles. These include reports on a business language centre in a CTC, electronic recording of achievement and electronic student registration (the use of swipe cards), the extended school day, the implementation of information technology in the curriculum, and the use of technology to combat truancy. For further information, contact: Yvonne Plows, Secretarial Services Manager, CTC Trust Ltd, 9 Whitehall, London SW1A 2DD (Tel: +71 839 9339; Fax: +71 839 5898).

School and the community

There are obvious educational benefits to be gained from schools' use of community resources, such as museums and libraries, as well as from the involvement of parents and others in supporting teaching in schools.

Benefits also accrue from the use by local communities of school premises, including the more cost-effective use of public resources, the enrichment of social life (there may be no alternative venue for events), and increased familiarity with schools which may lead to support for their work, for example, through mentoring, fund-raising, the offer of work placements. Vandalism may decrease and, where there are youth recreational or other facilities, such as those for childcare, there may be a reduction in other neighbourhood problems. By catering for all young people, schools promote democracy and social integration rather than separation and exclusion.

COMMUNITY USE

TECHNOLOGY IN CURRICULUM

SCHOOL MANAGEMENT

VOCATIONAL EDUCATION

REMODELLING BUILDINGS

Integrated Lyceums in Greece

Between 1984 and 1989, the Greek government introduced a new type of secondary school, the 'integrated lyceum', which would offer 14-17 year-olds a route either to higher education or vocational qualification (after an extra, fourth year).

Established in cities nationwide, the integrated lyceums aim to:

● broaden and modernise the content of general education to give all students a grounding in theoretical and practical studies;

● promote the socialisation of pupils within the school community through a democratic organisation, including the involvement by student committees in the management of the school, and the opportunity to take part in a wide range of optional social and cultural activities; and

● restore the school's links with its community.

Measures taken to achieve these aims would include:

● inviting individuals with special knowledge and skills, and representatives of community organisations, into schools to contribute to teaching and other activities;

● encouraging local companies and other employers to provide opportunities for experience and project work, as part of vocational guidance and counselling, to help students consider career choices;

● arranging educational visits to museums, libraries, companies, and technical and cultural institutions, and involving students in the design and creation of community facilities such as youth centres and libraries; and

125

● providing non-compulsory cultural and sports activities, run in-school and aimed at the development of the personality of the students.

The lyceums offer a three-year curriculum for students aged 14-17 which comprises a minimum of 34 hours' studies a week (30 weeks a year). There are common (core) subjects and electives, with progressive specialisation in the second and third years. Extra optional subjects are provided, beyond the basic requirement.

Of special note are:

● the introduction of new common subjects into the curriculum, including technology and production (first year, five hours a week), which involves study of the history of technology and industrial processes, and laboratory and workshop activities carried out individually and in teams, and information technology studies (second year, two hours a week);

● twenty-two optional subjects – of which students can choose no more than two – covering a wide range of the arts, additional foreign languages and information technology studies, athletics and sociology subjects (particular subjects are offered provided at least 10 pupils request them);

● three of the six second-year courses involve different aspects of technology (mechanical, electrical, chemical), each with a common element of about 50 per cent maths, physics and chemistry;

● in the third year 17 courses are offered, ranging from administrative-secretarial services to librarianship, medical laboratory work to social welfare, as well as a broad range of technologies, pure science, the humanities and applied arts courses; and

● still further specialisation leading to vocational (as opposed to pre-vocational) qualification is available in some subject areas for those wishing to continue into a fourth year at the lyceums.

New Philadelphia Integrated Lyceum, Athens

The facilities requirements of the new lyceums were extensive. Apart from the necessary classrooms, a considerable number of laboratories and social activities spaces had to be created. The quality of the facilities was regarded as an important factor in reflecting the school's purpose.

It was decided that the lyceums would be housed in existing buildings, after alteration. In practice, about half of the assigned buildings had been recently built, and were spacious enough to require only minor adjustment, but the remainder were old buildings, often in a bad condition. Planning the new schools in premises currently being used by other schools posed particular technical problems.

New Philadelphia is a working class suburb in the north of Athens and has one of the biggest school complexes in the city. At the time work on creating the

BEFORE

primary   lower secondary   general lyceum

unused space   technical and vocational

AFTER

primary   lower secondary

integrated lyceum   technical and vocational

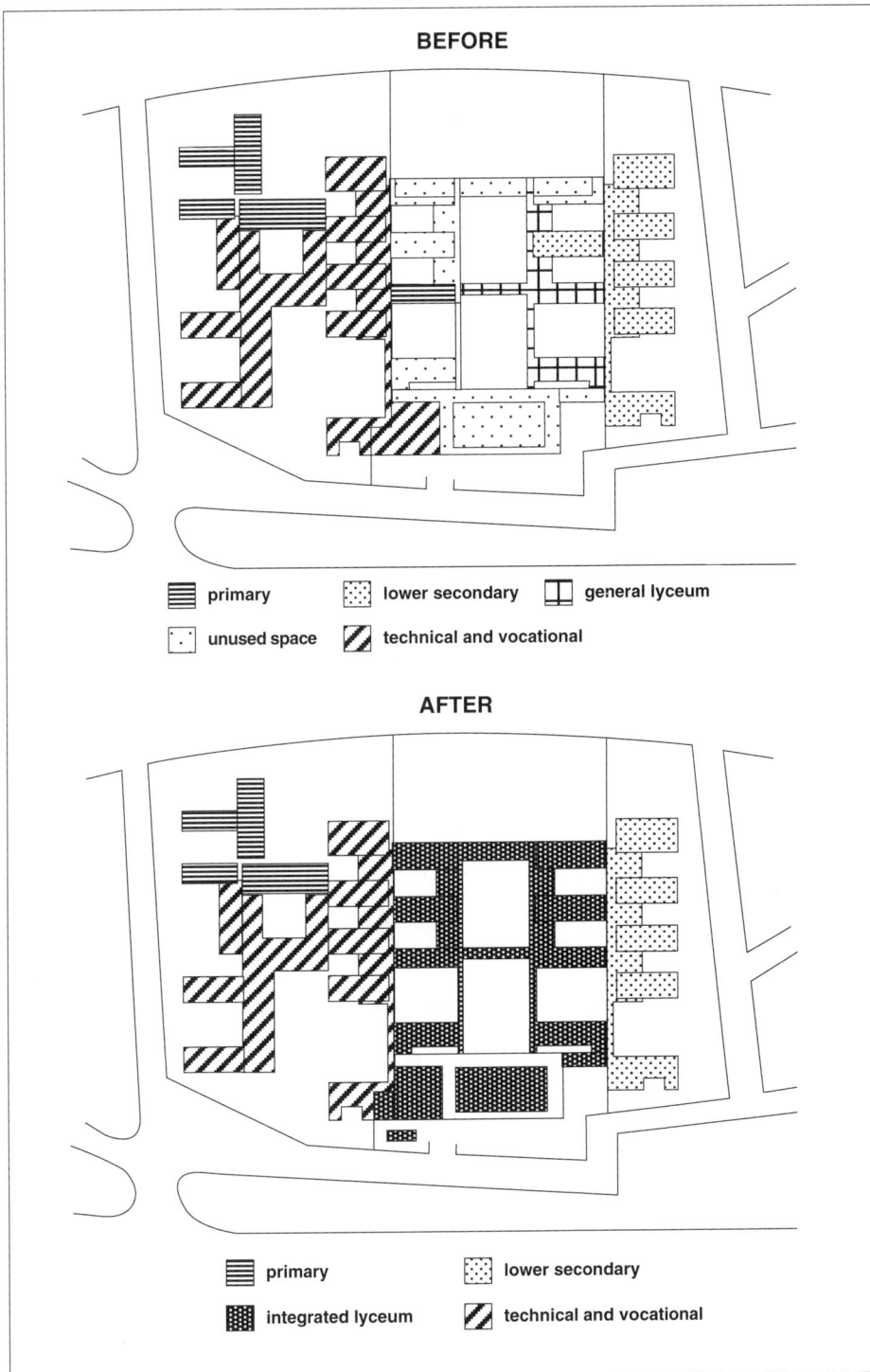

The New Philadelphia building complex before and after renewal (1983-88), showing the allocation of space to different types of education, and how the central part of the complex became the integrated lyceum.

127

lyceums began, it comprised two elementary schools, two middle schools, three technical and vocational schools (one for evening studies only) and one general high school. Part of the premises designated for the new lyceum belonged to the high school, which was to be gradually merged with the lyceum, although both would co-exist for two years.

Given this situation, and the short deadline for the lyceum's opening (only six months from the start of the project), some of the planning arrangements necessarily had to be temporary, and the accent put on flexible and low cost solutions. Working with teachers, who were developing curricula, and the new school's administration, architects had to assemble a plan which entailed the study and implementation of a variety of factors, including:

● minor repairs (broken windows, etc.);

● the rearrangement of functions and spaces;

● demolitions, new walls and utility connections;

● improvement of the quality of the premises, both inside and outdoors;

● conversion of classrooms to laboratories; and

● construction of a new three-storey annex.

Work started three months before the opening of the school and was completed in four phases.

Phase I: The first adjustment operations provided the necessary rooms for the function of 10 first year classes – 10 classrooms, two laboratories for technology and production, a gymnasium, an auditorium, a multi-use hall, and two offices.

Phase II: Space requirements for the second year classes were covered with the acquisition of new rooms (nine classrooms, a second auditorium, seven laboratories and a library), while improvements and space reallocation in anticipation of the third year were effected for the building as a whole.

Phase III: In third year, the high school was totally merged and its space fully allocated to the lyceum, which acquired seven more classrooms. Planning began on the annex.

Phase IV: During the fourth and fifth years of implementation, the annex was constructed so that the lyceum eventually comprised 44 classrooms and 18 laboratories as well as the auditoriums and offices.

The total costs were about $60 000 for the renewal and adaptation, and $700 000 for the annex. The school occupies 8 000 square metres (86 000 sq ft), and currently has 1 080 students and 95 teachers.

During the year many events take place in the school to which the public is invited, including a two-day festival. Laboratories and auditoriums are widely used by other schools, the parents' association, the municipality, and scientific and other organisations. Some other spaces are used for teacher education classes.

The physical environment has improved. Damage is always repaired; both indoor and outdoor spaces have been 'greened', for example with flower pots in classrooms and hallways; several classes each year volunteer to paint their classrooms; and a scheme promoting student mural paintings has helped to eliminate graffiti and vandalism.

The Integrated Lyceum, a 60-page booklet (in English), is available free from the Ministry of National Education and Religion. Contact: Nassie Xanalatou, Ministry of National Education and Religion, Mitropoleos 15, Athens 101 85, Greece (Tel: +1 32 46 235; Fax: +1 32 20 644).

Dealing with an urban problem — vandalism

The effects of theft and criminal damage – vandalism and arson – disrupt the daily work of schools and help to drain maintenance and repair budgets. Where left unattended, they produce a blighted environment which diminishes student and community pride in schools, and may deter people from using them.

Research in the United Kingdom shows that about 10 per cent of school districts' maintenance budgets is committed annually to repairing damage caused by arson and vandalism, and in one case in four vandalism results in lost teaching time (especially in elementary schools). The costs incurred in big city districts are about three times higher than the national average.

The Martin Luther King School, Haarlem

Haarlem is the capital of the province of North Holland, in the Netherlands, and has a population of 150 000. The Martin Luther King School was built in the 1960s, and since 1970 had been prey to continual vandalism. As one police officer remarked: "Everything these kids can possibly do to wreck a building, they've done to the M.L. King school!"

The school consists of a complex of buildings on a site 175 by 50 metres (8 750 square metres; 94 180 square feet). On one side of the complex is a nursery (kindergarten) and primary school. On the other is a gymnasium and an annex to the primary school. Between these clusters of buildings are a playground and several grassed areas. A sports centre runs along the length of the complex on one side; houses line the other. The two shorter sides of the complex are occupied by streets, and the school grounds are used as a thoroughfare by pedestrians and cyclists.

Failure

From 1970 to 1987, the school was subject to repeated vandalism and arson. Walls were defaced and sometimes as many as 40 windows broken in a single night; surrounding sidewalks were torn up and used as ammunition. Students often had to cross a carpet of broken glass to reach classrooms, and the schoolday would begin with the clearance of debris. On one occasion, the school's archives were destroyed by a fire bomb.

In addition, vandals used bicycle stands as ladders and cycled on the school's flat roofs, and playground equipment, telephone wires, locks and doors were repeatedly damaged. Teachers were threatened with violence, parents attending school events had their cars damaged, and local residents who complained to

Students often had to cross a carpet of broken glass to reach classrooms. The day would begin with the clearance of debris.

the police had their windows smashed. The cost of damage during the period exceeded $500 000.

Many steps were taken to try to abate this tide of vandalism. Prior to vacations thick wooden boards were nailed across the windows; special 'lexan' glass (five times stronger than ordinary glass and costing $150 a window) was installed, only to be successfully attacked with wooden beams; a high metal fence was erected, and repeatedly broken down; regular police patrols were instituted, but caught few vandals 'red handed'; the gymnasium was kept open after hours for community use; buildings were repainted; and teachers and parents sometimes spent the night on the premises to keep watch. Only the installation of a 'silent alarm', linked to the local fire department, had any noticeable effect – in minimising the effects of arson.

Success

By the mid-1980s, Haarlem was third among the Netherlands' "most unsafe cities". Each year, one out of every two citizens was the victim of crime of one sort or another. Incidents of vandalism were increasing. As a result, the city council decided traditional approaches – focused on policing and the criminal justice system – were insufficient. An integrated, multi-agency strategy was designed, and a crime prevention office created under the jurisdiction of the mayor.

Vandals used bicycle stands as ladders and cycled on the school's flat roofs

Following meetings between teachers, parents, police, members of the neighbourhood council and representatives of local government public works and urban renewal agencies, a new plan was adopted to combat vandalism at the Martin Luther King School. This comprised:

● Remodelling of the school grounds. A lower, 1.2 metres (4 feet) high perimeter fence replaced the old one, and was bordered on the inside by prickly burberry bushes – the aim being to make the school grounds less accessible without giving the school the appearance of a fortress (which, it was felt, would only challenge vandals). Outside the fence, a well-lit path was laid, to provide an alternative thoroughfare to the former one through the school grounds.

● School gardens were created, to increase students' involvement and sense of ownership in relation to the premises. Also, an anti-vandalism programme was run in the school in conjunction with the police. (Similar programmes are now run in most elementary schools every year. The experience of doing so has been incorporated in a crime prevention catalogue – an ideas and advice guide – to help teachers increase students' concern and responsibility about crime, which is now used in all Haarlem schools.)

● Local residents were encouraged to notify the police immediately if they sensed trouble in the vicinity of the school, and steps were taken by the police to ensure confidentiality. Additional surveillance was provided by the employment of a caretaker who would also undertake minor repairs.

● Perpetrators, if caught, would have to pay immediately for damage resulting from their vandalism.

The plan cost $90 000 to implement, and it has been so successful that this investment was recouped in expenditure savings within two years. Overall, in Haarlem, the annual cost of vandalism to municipal property, including schools, has been more than halved, to $250 000. Crime has decreased, so that one in three Haarlemmers a year is a victim – still high but much closer to the national figure of 27 per cent (1989), as reported in victimisation surveys. Five years on from the launch of the plan and the Martin Luther King School continues to remain free of vandalism, so that, in 1993, the authorities felt confident in installing new playground equipment.

City officials believe the key to success in tackling crime and vandalism has been the adoption of an approach which is:

● integrated – combining physical, spatial and social measures;

● multi-agency – drawing on wider expertise and participation, and creating a broader sense of ownership;

● offensive and constructive, rather than defensive by relying on policing and fortification;

● positive – clean and well-kept environments deter vandalism, those left in a state of disrepair encourage it; and

A high metal fence was erected in a defensive response to vandalism. It was repeatedly broken down.

● problem-solving and systematic – for example, all building plans are now checked against criteria for crime prevention.

In the new plan, the height of the fence was lowered and a well-lit path created

Contact: Kees Roos, Bureau Veiligheid, Gemeente Haarlem, Postbus 511, 2003 PB Haarlem, Netherlands (Tel: +23 17 12 12; Fax: +23 32 06 15).

A series of publications offering guidance and information about crime prevention in schools is published by the UK government. Available from HMSO (see CTC case study) are four in the *Building Bulletins* series: *67 Crime Prevention in Schools: Practical Guidance*, 1987, price £4.95; *69 Specification, Installation and Maintenance of Intruder Alarm Systems*, 1989, price £7.50; *75 CCTV Surveillance*, 1991, price £5.00; and *78 Security Lighting*, 1993, price £4.25. Available free from Department for Education Publications, PO Box 2193, London E15 2EU (Tel: +81 533 2000; Fax: +81 533 7700) are *Design Note 48: Graffiti Removal and Control*, 1989; *Architects and Building Paper 15: Lockers and Secure Storage*, 1990; *Broadsheet 28: School Glazing and Vandalism*, 1992; and *Sprinklers in Schools*, 1993. Also published with government support is: *How to Combat Arson in Schools*, price £2, from Arson Prevention Bureau, 140 Aldersgate Street, London EC1A 4DD.

A CITY-WIDE RENOVATION INITIATIVE

The scale of the repair backlog may be too great to be eliminated by incremental improvements brought about through the use of existing or even augmented budgets: it may require a comprehensive improvement programme to 'wipe the slate clean'. But, as a French city which launched a major intervention, in 1989, concluded, such an initiative needs to lead to serious consideration of measures to ensure that adequate, ongoing maintenance is then achieved.

The city of Lyon

Lyon sits astride France's principal commercial route – from Paris to the Mediterranean. Also downstream from Geneva on the River Rhône, it is an industrial city, historically famous for its silk products, and, with nearly half a million inhabitants, the nation's second largest.

As with many European cities, postwar reconstruction, the baby boom and decolonisation (more than a million French people left Algeria on independence, in 1962) combined to create an acute building need, which resulted in a construction boom between the mid-1950s and early 1970s. Also as elsewhere, haste, apparent 'cheapness' through the use of industrial construction methods, massive scale and vulgar aesthetics were hallmarks of this boom, whose legacy in terms of premature and expensive repair has been increasingly felt in the last decade.

(In Britain, which has a similar history, the National Audit Office reported, regarding schools, in 1991, that: "The emergency repairs now necessary are the primary reason why authorities have had to divert funds from the routine maintenance of older buildings. As the cycle of replacement and renewal of stock has yet to reach its peak, the unit costs of maintenance in real terms are likely to continue to rise until around the year 2000.")

Lyon also has many newer immigrants, and the need for their social integration is another starting point for the decision by the mayor, Michel Noir, elected in 1989, to use his six-year mandate to prioritise measures which would benefit children, particularly those aged three to nine.

One initiative involves bringing all the elementary schools in the city (high schools are administered at *département* or county level) to new minimum maintenance and accommodation standards. Says Christiane Nicolas, of the mayor's office: "By 1995, all children in Lyon, without exception, will go to school in buildings which are comfortable and comforting, functional, and favourable to their physical and intellectual development."

Conversion of a room to create a library with mezzanine at Delorme elementary school.

Task and means

Lyon's inventory of pre-schools (ages 3-6) and elementary schools (ages 6-11) comprises 210 schools, occupying 20.2 hectares (50 acres) and consisting of 300 000 square metres (3.23 m sq. ft.) of floor area, two-thirds of which is teaching space. The enrolment is a little more than 33 000 students. The dates and types of construction vary considerably, and include traditional style buildings in stone, wood-framed ones with tile roofs, and those built in concrete and pre-fabrication materials.

The cost of the improvement programme over the four years to 1993 was expected to be about $34 million. A first set of credits totalling almost half this amount was set aside in 1989.

Management of the programme is being carried out by a team of 41 employees which comprises a technical and building department within the city administration. Private consultants are commissioned to provide design services.

Elements of the programme

To bring buildings to the minimum standard involved:

● bringing electrical and technical installations and equipment up to date;

● general renovation work, improving acoustics, ensuring thermal insulation;

● cleaning façades and integrating them into the surrounding environment;

● repairing and improving courtyards, playgrounds and their equipment;

● functional improvements called for by new teaching methods;

● effecting savings through measures such as water conservation, achieved in particular by repairing bathrooms and toilets;

● improving the security of part of buildings most susceptible to theft and break-ins; and

● providing access for students with physical disabilities.

Taking account of new needs in schools entailed:

● creation of libraries/ documentation centres;

● creation of audio-visual rooms, installation of cables and the adaptation of technical equipment;

● development of medical care services, including the creation or renovation of in-school medical care centres and equipment;

● provision of laboratories for learning languages, music rooms, sports facilities and equipment (gymnasiums, climbing walls, dance rooms, etc.), and school meals facilities (174 cafeterias); and

● general improvement of comfort and functionality, including redistributing water supply points in pre-schools, improving acoustics, lighting and room distribution.

Outcomes

The programme sought to make a 'major intervention' in its first year, with additional work being carried out in subsequent years. To this end, a survey of inventory was carried out (it took two weeks) and 163 initial projects agreed. These were put together with the help of 15 architects, 10 interior designers and 15 specialists on financial issues relating to buildings.

During the summer vacation (1989) work was carried out by 105 companies, and included construction of 75 libraries, 88 audio-visual rooms, three school cafeterias, 17 medical care centres, four gymnasiums, the cabling and networking of 25 schools, renovation of nearly 48 000 square metres (516 700 sq. ft.) of accommodation, the cleaning of about the same area of facades, and renovation and equipping of 12 200 square metres (131 300 sq. ft.) of playgrounds and courtyards.

Christiane Nicolas comments on the experience gained:

"This major operation of upgrading the entire building stock has led to serious reflection on what policy should be adopted, and used, to ensure that the quality now being obtained is maintained. The conclusion is that it is necessary to set aside an annual investment corresponding to 1.5 per cent of

Creation of a covered walkway between two buildings at Aveyron school.

A new extension at the J. Racine school

the value of a new building (in real terms) in order to ensure at least the minimum necessary upkeep and maintenance."

"One might justifiably claim that the all-out renovation project is a fine example of a comprehensive renewal of the city's building stock. But the lesson to be learned is that it is much better to implement a coherent policy of yearly work programmes, covered by a modest budget, than to inject massive amounts of funds on an irregular basis when problems become too severe."

"The users of the buildings and the population in general have given a positive response to the city's efforts. The effects of the project are particularly being felt in the less favoured neighbourhoods of the city, where other social programmes have often been implemented in conjunction with the renovation work carried out on the schools."

The current annual maintenance budget, excluding major (capital) works, is about $6.3 million ($180 per student).

Réussite scolaire, la Ville de Lyon rénove is a booklet containing brief information and more than 100 colour photographs regarding the city's school renovation and improvement programme. It and other information, including the newsletter *Info Ecole*, can be obtained from Christiane Nicolas, Hotel de Ville de Lyon, 69001 Lyon, France (Tel: +78 37 56 83). The National Audit Office report, *Repair and Maintenance of School Buildings*, is available, price £5.80 from HMSO Publications Centre, PO Box 276, London SW8 5DT, United Kingdom (Tel. orders: +71 873 9090; Tel. enquiries: +71 873 0011; Fax orders: +71 873 8200; Fax enquiries: +71 873 8463).

APPROACHES TO MAINTENANCE

Maintenance is a key concern for urban school districts, many of which have to cope with an inheritance of old and unsuitable buildings at a time of rising environmental and educational standards, and of fundamental changes in technologies.

In this case study, the sheer scale of the repair problem facing Chicago provides some pointers to reform. Milwaukee and New Jersey are a city and state currently improving their planning and funding arrangements, and the city of New York is improving the condition of its schools through biannual classroom inspections using hand-held computers.

Chicago

Bruce Berndt, president of Chicago Principals Association, recalls that, in 23 years as a school principal in the city, "I remember being on deferred maintenance most of [the] time". And he adds: "You can be on deferred maintenance only so long before it starts coming down around your head."

Chicago is the United States' third largest public school system, with more than 400 000 students attending just over 600 schools and 45 400 employees (of which 24 290 are teachers).

The budget for the year ending September 1991 was $2.25 billion, of which 48 per cent came from city revenues, nearly 39 per cent from the State of Illinois, and the rest from the federal government. The amount earmarked for school repairs and maintenance was $240 million. Of this, $63 million was for maintenance, accounting for 2.8 per cent of planned spending – the largest proportion since 1973 (the lowest was 1.4 per cent).

By any standards, the city's school buildings are old. Almost half of the schools were built before 1930, including more than 80 in the last century, and fewer than one-third were constructed in the last 30 years. (This compares with, say, Baltimore – also one of the United States' oldest cities – where the average age of school buildings is 30 years.)

The city estimates it would cost $1.075 billion to carry out the repairs and new construction necessary to bring school buildings up to an acceptable standard. Two-thirds are in "dire need" of repair, according to James Haney, the city's school facilities director. Almost a hundred schools each require more than $1 million spending on them.

But the high cost of repair is only one indication of past neglect. On any one day there are an estimated 900 fire and building code violations in schools (on average school board officials appear in court on a new case involving a violation once a week). Each month repair workers respond to some 1 200 building 'emergencies' – ones which pose a threat to student safety or the continued operation of a school (typical are broken boilers, burst water pipes and electrical failures) – and the backlog at any one time consists of more than a thousand repairs.

Schools used to be painted once every eight years, but the painting cycle has had to be abandoned, and, since 1971, the number of workers in the school board's maintenance pool has been cut by 36 per cent (to 323 workers), while the number of school premises has increased by 15 per cent.

Issues

The situation in Chicago highlights a number of important aspects of the maintenance problem.

● Low budget priority. School building budgets have been repeatedly raided to help meet the cost of wage settlements (between 1969 and 1991 teachers successfully went on strike for higher pay nine times).

● Tax resistance. Despite urging by school board officials, politicians have been reluctant to ask city residents and businesses to pay more in local taxes. The size of the facilities problem is now too great to afford remedy by a single tax increase. Even with an increase, money would have to be borrowed – thus incurring long-term debt charges.

● The powers of principals. Dating from the days when schools had high-pressure boiler heating systems, each has a city-certified 'school engineer', with equal status to the principal and who works independently. Principals cannot order repairs, hire or fire custodians (junior school-based maintenance staff), or oversee repair work.

● Union resistance. The high-pressure boilers have gone but the engineers have fought off attempts to eliminate their jobs and make school-based maintenance the responsibility of custodians. Union rules (and insurance liability problems) have prohibited parental, and other do-it-yourself repairs in schools.

● High public works costs. Maintenance staff are relatively well-paid, in 1991 earning about $23 an hour (nearly six times the national minimum wage). Overtime is paid at 'time and a half' or 'double time' if past noon on Saturdays or on Sundays. Unit costs of repairs are also high, for example, to replace a sash window costs $1000, to replace a flourescent light fitting $125, to install a toilet for the disabled $11 000, and to replace an exterior door $2 400.

● School-based management. Chicago spent $97 million in 1991 on salaries for school engineers, school-based custodians and personnel in its maintenance pool (the engineers cost about $30 million). This was equivalent to $161 000 per school or $240 per student. Nor do these figures include the labour costs of outside contractors, who carry out about 40 per cent of emergency repairs – let alone the cost of materials. Some argue repairs would be quicker, and money spent more cost-effectively, if schools managed their own facility budgets.

Milwaukee

Ninety miles north of Chicago, Milwaukee is a city of 630 000 people (about a quarter of the size of Chicago), which is making a concerted effort to tackle maintenance as part of a rolling, 10-year capital programme which addresses both new space needs – the expansion of capacity – and the need to maintain existing facilities (the preservation of capacity).

Milwaukee has more than 200 education buildings, including 153 schools, comprising over 18 million sq. ft. of space (167.2 hectares) and seven million sq. ft. (650 320 sq. metres) of roof area. The district encompasses 100 square miles (259 sq. km.), and the school board has 10 000 full-time employees, of which 1 200 are engaged in facilities administration and repair.

Present

For 1992/93 the schools budget was $650 million, of which $50 million was spent on 'facilities', although only 38 per cent of this ($19 m) was allocated to building and construction work (as opposed to wages).

Of this $19 million, $14.9 million was earmarked for expansion projects – mostly on a major renovation of a middle school and a new elementary and new middle school. This left $4.1 million to be spent on the preservation of existing buildings.

Preservation comprises six elements: spending on deferred maintenance; major maintenance projects; remodelling; school security; energy conservation; and costs associated with code compliance (for example, meeting regulations regarding asbestos, the use of underground storage tanks, and the integration of people with disabilities). The proportion of the total schools budget devoted to these items was less than two-thirds of one per cent (0.63 per cent).

Future

The master plan for the decade to 2002 involves significant changes in this pattern of funding, specifically: a switch of resources away from expansion and towards preservation; holding spending constant in real terms; and, a shift within the preservation category to maintenance from security and energy conservation.

Thus, in 1994/95, when the new pattern of allocations is expected to be in place, spending on preservation will comprise four-fifths of the non-wages facilities budget, and expansion one-fifth, reversing the current proportions; preservation will account for 2.7 per cent of the total school spending; and deferred and major maintenance will comprise just over 60 per cent of spending in the preservation category, compared to somewhat less than 40 per cent, currently. (Concomitantly, the proportions spent on school security and on energy conservation are projected to fall from 15.2 per cent to 7.2 per cent, and 23.5 per cent to 4.3 per cent, respectively.)

Ed McMilin, facility planner for Milwaukee Public Schools, says the aim is to implement a sustained strategy for maintenance for which "the five C's" will be watchwords:

● Commitment – from the school board and senior management to achieve the goals of the plan; the involvement of all district personnel, not only the facilities staff; and the provision of the appropriate personnel and financial resources to implement the programme.

● Comprehensive – tackling the problem on a broad front, covering all building elements and equipment, including compliance with all mandated and code requirements ($21 million is projected to be spent on asbestos removal over nine years); addressing all types of maintenance including deferred maintenance; containing a high quality cleaning programme; and being part of an overall facilities strategy.

● Consistent – implementing the plan on a rolling basis.

● Continuous – effecting the provisions of the plan annually and without new hiatuses which would cause the maintenance backlog to grow again.

● Creative – being responsive to new ideas, financing arrangements, and management techniques.

The identification of sources of funding is essential. At present prices, the total cost of implementing the plan is $195.7 million (of which $160.7 million is on preservation). Slightly less than 20 per cent will be found from city property tax revenues, and about the same amount in the early years will be raised from borrowing. The public will be asked to approve additional taxes to cover the remaining 62 per cent – $48.6 million for deferred maintenance and $72.3 million for other preservation elements of the plan.

Nevertheless, whatever the outcome of a ballot, implementation of the programme will go forward. As McMilin says: "The 10-year capital plan is a guide for implementing an overall facilities strategy. It is not a static process, but one which is flexible and always changing to meet the current conditions and circumstances. As long as changes to it take the five C's into consideration, it will always be a viable document."

New Jersey

A facilities master plan, of course, is not sufficient, even if frequently updated and revised: the State of New Jersey requires five-year plans of its school districts, as part of a quinquennial monitoring exercise, but research in 1990 found that the outstanding school construction need for the state was $1.8 billion – and one-third could be attributed to deferred maintenance.

A 1991 survey of schools in the largest school district, the city of Newark, indicated that two in five schools were in poor condition externally, and the same proportion in a similar condition internally.

Background

New Jersey is the only state defined as wholly urban by the US Census Bureau. It is also the most densely populated, with 7.7 million people living in an area about three-quarters that of Belgium. In fact, by far the majority live in the 70-mile long conurbation on the opposite bank of the Hudson River to New York.

Almost 40 per cent of public school students in the state live in households below the federal poverty line. The gap between rich and poor areas is large and reflected in school district revenues. Also, there are very many districts – nearly 600 (of which one in six has fewer than 300 students).

Urban school districts argued that funding disparities between themselves and suburban districts adversely affected the quality of education they could provide, and successfully challenged the state in court. This led to the passage of the Quality Education Act, in 1990, which defines a 'quality education' and establishes a per student state-wide baseline for school expenditure.

The court did not rule specifically on facilities, giving the general direction that "a thorough and efficient education requires adequate facilities... while it is possible that the richest of educations can be conferred in the rudest of surroundings, the record in this case demonstrates that deficient facilities are conducive to a deficient education". However, subsequently, the Act laid down a recommended level for facilities spending of $110 per student per annum.

Concurrent to the court case (which lasted 10 years), the state legislature set up the Commission on Business Efficiency of the Public Schools. In turn, this commissioned New Jersey Institute of Technology to carry out a study on school facilities, which was published in November 1990. This raised a number of additional issues.

Issues

● Monitoring. The state requirement for district facility 'master plans' was only partially accompanied by review of facility conditions and management procedures; mostly it served as a watchdog for compliance to building and other (statutory) codes. While deferred maintenance was identified after a period of time, there was no method of assuring that buildings were consistently maintained.

Monitoring would be improved, it was concluded, if it were linked to technical assistance. However, this should not be restricted to cases of non-compliance to codes, should be adequately resourced (including staff training), and supported by tools such as state guidebooks.

● Co-ordination. The state's requirements and procedures did not "work together as a system" nor produce "a focused effort in regard to school maintenance".

This would be improved if criteria were laid down for maintenance and capital improvements, and state funding linked to the achievement of objectives and priorities. Also, there should be proper review of mandatory planning documents, and a systematic evaluation of districts' needs.

● Effectiveness. At the local level there was often a mismatch between planning and funding. Maintenance budgets were regarded as low priority items, and the quinquennial monitoring cycle resulted in booms and slumps, with districts increasing their efforts prior to monitoring and slackening them afterwards.

To effect a better link between planning and funding, it was suggested that New Jersey should consider direct appropriation of funds for school building maintenance, or require that a maintenance element be included in local budgets.

New Jersey is currently pursuing implementation of some of these changes. However, the commission was not able to support the study team's recommendation for a system to ensure the "steady-state" funding of maintenance. "While laudable... [it is] not feasible given the current financial condition of the state," it concluded.

New York

With over one million students attending its nearly 1 000 public schools, facilities management in New York is on a grand scale. There are, for example, more than 9 000 student toilets and washrooms to maintain, as well as 47 000 classrooms, in a portfolio of assets whose worth runs into billions of dollars.

Like other cities, however, New York's budget for upkeep of its schools has been perpetually under pressure. The picture for classrooms in 1989 included 35 per cent with one or more lights missing or flickering; 66 per cent of storage closets and lockers damaged; 40 per cent with at least one window pane missing or broken (and one in three curtains missing or damaged); 34 per cent with doors defective; and 73 per cent with some furniture broken or missing.

Scorecard

To make a dent in the problem, it was crucial to have detailed and up-to-date information on the state of facilities, and to help achieve this New York introduced a new computer-based management information system – school scorecard – in 1987. This enables a team of 10 field inspectors, using hand-held computers, to report on the physical appearance of every classroom in the 970 schools twice a year.

This information is then uploaded onto the system's local area network, where it can be analysed to identify needs and help establish priorities for the schools' six monthly maintenance plan. It also enables monitoring through time of the effectiveness of repair programmes, as well as providing the data for an ongoing city-wide facilities inventory.

Although focusing on perceptible damage and decay – the system measures conditions as experienced by students and teachers rather than attempting a technical assessment of the architectural integrity or mechanical systems of buildings – the system has proved invaluable in helping New York to spend its budget on cleaning and repairs fairly and wisely, says Tyra Liebmann, director of the School Scorecard Unit in the Division of Educational Facilities.

"Inspectors have repeatedly demonstrated, through rigorous testing procedures, that they are capable of making judgments about conditions in a very consistent manner," she says. "The system produces very accurate quantitative measurements of school building appearance that can be used to compare individual buildings to one another, profile entire districts, and summarize conditions on a city-wide basis."

Assessment

On visits to schools, members of the field team are prompted by the computers on the items and conditions to be inspected at each location. All classrooms, except those locked and withdrawn from use, are inspected, as are other teaching spaces, student toilets and washrooms, cafeterias and some administrative offices.

Appearance ratings on a seven-point scale are given for three key items, all applying to walls but only the first two to ceilings. The criteria are:

● material integrity – damage to structural material such as plaster, tiles and wood, including missing pieces, holes, rotting, and cracks;

● paint condition – surface blemishes, especially paint which is cracked, chipped, peeling or blistering; and

● dirt and grime – evidence of dust, graffiti, mismatched paint and material, adhesive tape and gum.

Scores range from zero – virtually no damage – to six. Anything above a 'two' denotes a very poor environment – a description applied to about 2 500 classrooms (5.3 per cent of the total) in the most recent annual scorecard report (whose figures average those for the two inspections carried out during the school year).

In addition to the appearance ratings, scorecard data include simple 'yes/no' statements about whether or not fixtures are damaged. A long checklist includes lights, radiators, floors, furniture, storage items, doors, windows and curtains, and chalkboards. There is another list for student toilets, covering sinks, urinals and WCs, partitions, toilet paper, soap, paper towels and floors.

'Scorecard' can also be used for ad hoc analyses and special projects, for example compiling inventories of, and ratings for, school playgrounds; surveys of the condition of student lockers in school corridors; qualitative studies of the effectiveness of contractors' work in specific schools; and ongoing reporting of work on hazardous conditions being undertaken by the city's Office of Building Services.

The scorecard unit is currently extending the system into computer modelling. Various data on building use and construction characteristics are being used to help predict what will happen to appearance ratings under a variety of alternative maintenance, managerial and renovation regimes.

Bruce Berndt and James Haney are quoted in *Schools in Ruins*, a reprint of a series of articles on educational facilities appearing in the *Chicago Sun-Times*, 14-18 April 1991. For Milwaukee, contact: Edward McMilin, Milwaukee Public Schools, 1124 N 11 Street, Milwaukee, Wisconsin 53233, USA (Tel: +414 283 4600; Fax: +414 283 4682). *New Jersey: Approaches to School Maintenance*, the report of a study by Susan Stuebing and others for the New Jersey Commission on Business Efficiency of the Public Schools, was published in 1990, price $10, by New Jersey Institute of Technology. It is also available on the ERIC library and information database. Contact: Susan Stuebing, New Jersey Institute of Technology, University Heights, Newark, New Jersey 07102, USA (Tel: +201 596 3097; Fax: +201 596 8443). The City of New York Board of Education publishes an annual *School Scorecard Report*, copies of which may be obtained free on request from Bruce Barret, School Scorecard Unit, Room 382, 122 Amsterdam Avenue, New York, New York 10023, USA (Tel: +212 877 1710; Fax: +212 721 2622).

Designing schools of the future

A new school opening its doors 30 years ago did so in a world in which there were no microprocessors, commercial telecommunications satellites and fibre optics; no wordprocessors, video cassette recorders and, even, pocket calculators; when the baby boom was at its peak, yet the boom in higher education had yet to occur, and most students left school, many unqualified, when they were 16 or younger.

What will schools be like 30 years hence? How can we plan for change? One city that has been searching for answers is Edinburgh.

New Leith Academy, Edinburgh

Edinburgh is the historic capital of Scotland and Britain's tenth largest city, with a population of nearly 450 000. Leith is the port for the city, situated on the east (North Sea) coast, and is an area of anticipated population growth. Education is the responsibility of Lothian Regional Council, one of the nine such council jurisdictions into which mainland Scotland (population five million) is divided.

The New Leith Academy is a new school built to replace the former Leith Academy. When it opened, in August 1991, it enrolled 900 students, but the building has been designed also for community use and can cater for as many as 1 500 people at any time. Most significantly, it has been designed to withstand anticipated, but as yet unforeseen, changes of use into the middle of the next century.

The construction of a new secondary school is a significant investment for the education authority and, in order to ensure that it represented a worthwhile use of resources, it was necessary to look beyond the building's use as a school and to think in terms of the creation of a long-term asset.

Few buildings are capable – during their 60-year lifespan – of responding to changes in user needs without becoming wholly or partially obsolescent, or else incurring very high costs for adaptation and extension. While the architects of New Leith Academy do not claim to have been able to foresee the changes that will take place, they have sought to identify broad areas from past events and current trends, and prodice a design which takes account of them.

The aim has been to synthesise local, national and international experience to provide the region with a building which will help, rather than hinder, the process of change throughout its life.

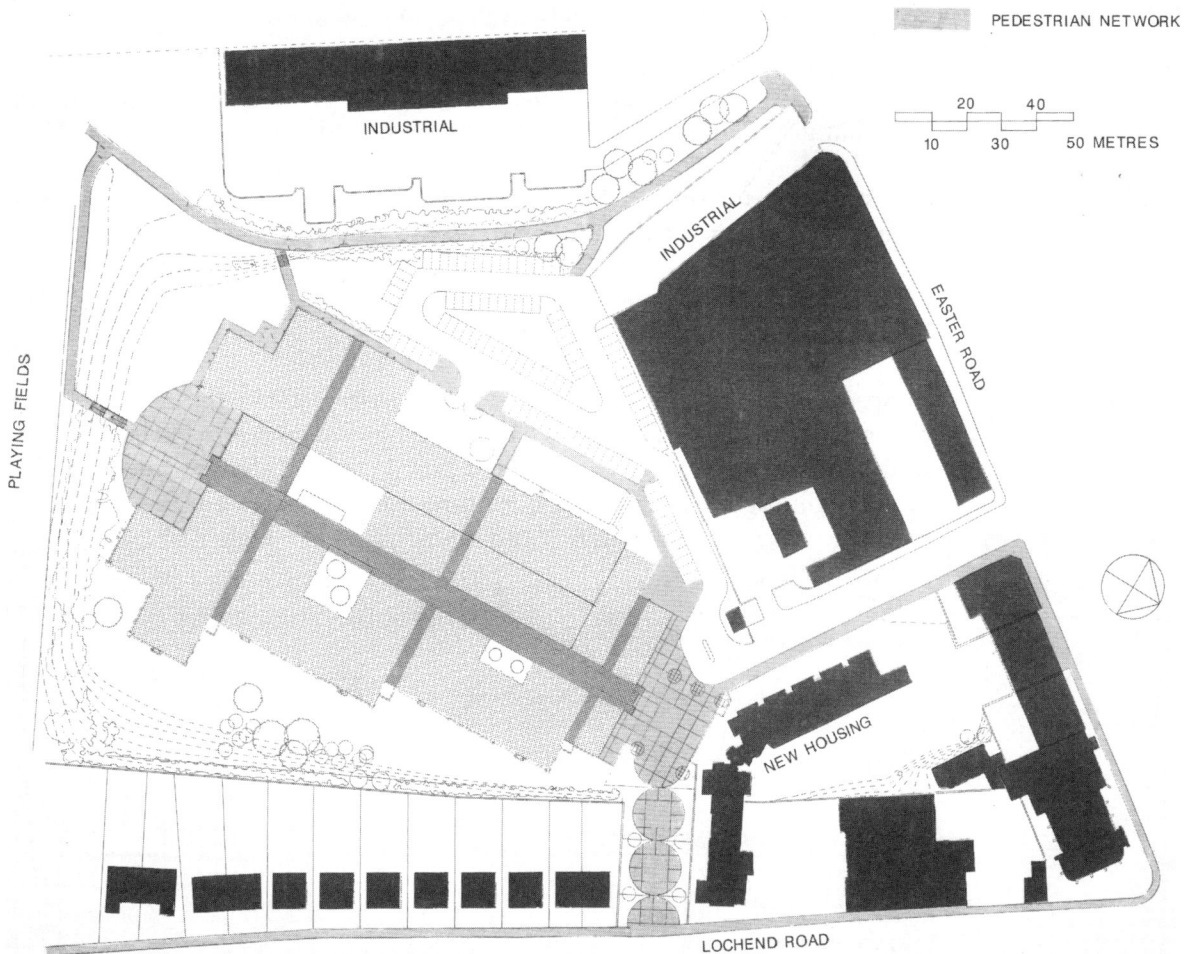

The site of New Leith Academy, showing adjacent land use and the public pedestrian areas.

Martin Garden, an architect with Lothian Regional Council, comments: "Maybe, in 20 or 30 years' time, when schools as we know them have ceased to exist, people will be popping into Leith Community Resource Centre for a swim, to give themselves an interactive medical examination, or to try out the latest virtual reality software...."

Characteristics of the new school

● The strategy for expansion and contraction which has been included in the design allows for growth of up to 40 per cent, or for radical contraction if educational demand should require.

● As a building with public access, the school includes some accommodation which is intended mainly for community use, and some where public access is possible without disrupting mainstream activities.

There are three kinds of circulation in the building, namely:

A central street – the building is planned like a shopping mall, with a glazed main street, with extensive planting, seats, a street cafe, displays, and festooned with hanging banners which indicate graphically the 'wares' on offer.

Side streets – these run at right angles to the main street, and which give access to any department without having to go through another one.

A tertiary circulation zone within each block of accommodation which may be a corridor or part of a larger space.

● Space has been planned to be versatile, so as to facilitate future curriculum changes. The range of space sizes has been simplified, and provided in a mixed distribution of open, partially open, and closed modes. Different types of space are brought together in groups. Furniture and fittings are not fixed in order to allow easy redeployment; and there is a comprehensive servicing infrastructure.

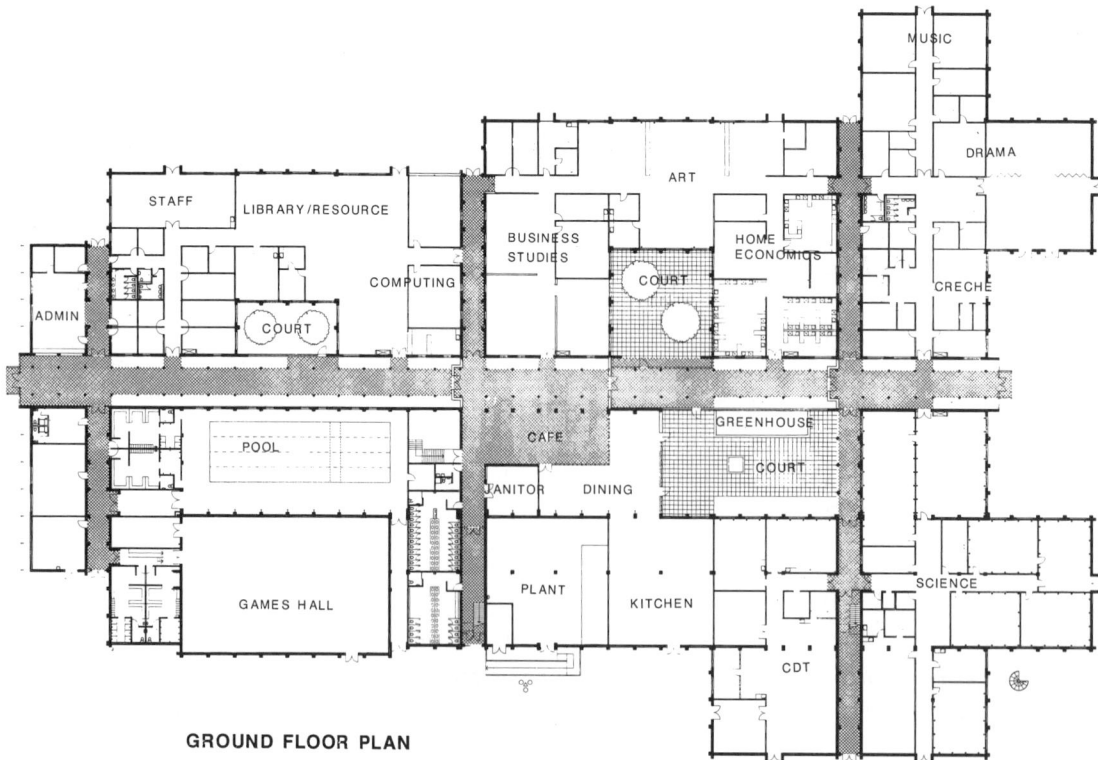

GROUND FLOOR PLAN

The ground floor plan of the school, with the circulation areas shaded

The school's central 'mall'.

● Allowance has been made for increased use of information technology. A network of cable and other servicing routes follows the circulation pattern. A comprehensive security system is provided.

● The likelihood of changes in teaching and learning methods has required special emphasis to be put on resource areas.

A central resource centre provides services to all activities within the school, as well as access to high-powered information technology equipment.

The library area within the central resource centre is a shared facility for school and public use, and incorporates provision for private study and open learning, while support facilities include a printing/reprographics unit, dark room, graphics studio, audio-visual production centre, hardware maintenance area with secure storage, and audio/video facilities for school-wide broadcasting.

Staff rooms and storage areas are located in each department, and offices, meeting and seminar rooms, and stores are situated throughout the building.

● The design reflects a shared school-and-community concept, based on four principles. These are that the building should not carry the institutionalised visual 'message' of many schools; it should be user-friendly for adults; it should have public access; and, through its design and quality, it should help foster pride on the part of users.

● As the building is complex and users requirements will change with increasing frequency, a user's manual has been developed as part of the facilities management strategy.

The building in use

"The building has been open for nearly two years now, and it works," says Martin Garden. Indeed, changes in community use and teaching requirements have already put its flexibility to the test. "Our experience has been to emphasise the need for great consideration to be given to strategic and tactical issues in building design while a project is at its conceptual stage. The project showed the need to educate intensively all members of the design team in maintaining the principles involved as design work progresses. Losing track of the principles and thus falling back on the habits and practices of the past is often tempting, but this must be avoided."

Contact: Martin Garden, Architecture and Design Centre, 181 Canongate, Royal Mile, Edinburgh, EH8 8BN, Scotland, United Kingdom (Tel: +31 556 1999; Fax: +31 557 1999).

CASE STUDY BIBLIOGRAPHY

'CCTV Surveillance', *Building Bulletin 75*; Her Majesty's Stationery Office, London, 1991.

Choice and Diversity: A New Framework for Schools; Her Majesty's Stationery Office, London, 1992.

Clynes, Roger. *Adaptability and Flexibility in Educational Facilities*; OECD/PEB, 1990.

'Crime Prevention in Schools: Practical Guidance', *Building Bulletin 67*; Her Majesty's Stationery Office, London, 1987.

'Educational Design Initiatives in City Technology Colleges,' *Building Bulletin 72*; Her Majesty's Stationery Office, London, 1990.

'Graffiti Removal and Control', *Design Note 48*; Department of Education and Science, London, 1989.

Hirsch, Donald. *The Learning City*; Gothenburg Education Committee, Sweden, 1993.

How to Combat Arson in Schools; Arson Prevention Bureau, London, 1993.

'Lockers and Secure Storage', *Architects and Building Paper 15*; Department of Education and Science, London, 1990.

Réussite scolaire, la Ville de Lyon rénove; Office of the Mayor, Lyon, France, 1991.

'School Glazing and Vandalism', *Broadsheet 28*; Department of Education and Science, London,1992.

'Security Lighting', *Building Bulletin 78*; Her Majesty's Stationery Office, London, 1993.

'Specification, Installation and Maintenance of Intruder Alarm Systems', *Building Bulletin 69*; Her Majesty's Stationery Office, London, 1989.

Sprinklers in Schools; Department for Education, London, 1993.

Stuebing Susan et al. *New Jersey: Approaches to School Maintenance*; report for the New Jersey Commission on Business Efficiency of the Public Schools; New Jersey Institute of Technology, Newark, 1990.

The Essential Educational Characteristics of a CTC Style School; the City Technology Colleges Trust, London, 1994.

The Integrated Lyceum; Ministry of National Education and Religion, Athens, 1989.

The National Audit Office, *Repair and Maintenance of School Buildings*; Her Majesty's Stationery Office, London, 1991.

'The Victoria Centre, Crewe: An Update', *Architects and Building Paper 8*; Department of Education and Science, London, 1985.

ALSO AVAILABLE

The Educational Infrastructure in Rural Areas

Rural schools in industrialised countries are frequently threatened with closure. They are either considered too small to offer a full educational experience, or are perceived as being too expensive to maintain. But closing the village school only accelerates the process of decline. Co-operation, clustering — whether formal or informal — and the use of new technologies can all offer ways to relieve the isolation of small schools. This report, which summarises discussion at a recent PEB seminar, examines some of the strategies available to school administrators and designers for redefining the role of educational facilities in rural areas.

(95 94 02 1) ISBN 92-64-14189-8, 36 pages. France: FF40. Other countries: FF50, US$9 or DM16.

Educational Facilities for Special Needs

More and more children with disabilities — physical or mental — are being educated in ordinary schools. The successful integration of pupils with special needs into the day-to-day life of the classroom will depend not only on the skill of teachers but also on the availability of appropriate facilities. This report gives advice on how school buildings can be designed, and existing ones adapted, to provide a welcoming and safe environment for all pupils, whatever their needs. It draws on examples of good practice and the experience of specialists from across the OECD area and will be a source of information for administrators, designers and teachers.

(95 94 01 1) ISBN 92-64-14098-0, 30 pages.

New Technology and its Impact on Educational Buildings

Written by Norman Willis, this publication describes what technology may have to offer and how it might change the learning process during the next twenty years. The review should help facility planners and school managers make informed decisions about what measures may improve their chances of introducing new technologies successfully and allow them to avoid potentially costly mistakes.

(02 92 15 1) ISBN 92-64-13756-4, 52 pages.

Decentralisation and Educational Building Management: The Impact of Recent Reforms

In OECD countries, recent moves to decentralise responsibility — from central government to local authorities, and from local authorities to schools themselves — have focused attention on the educational infrastructure and how it is managed. This report analyses the situation in a selected number of OECD countries and investigates how effective property management can improve the quality of educational systems.

(95 92 01 1) ISBN 92-64-13660-6, 88 pages.

Orders

All of the publications may be obtained directly from the OECD Publications and Information Centres or the main sales outlets for OECD publications listed on the following page. Payment may be made by cheque, money order or credit card (VISA, Mastercard, Eurocard). Prices are indicated in French Francs, US Dollars and German Marks. The distributor in your country will determine prices in local currency.

MAIN SALES OUTLETS OF OECD PUBLICATIONS
PRINCIPAUX POINTS DE VENTE DES PUBLICATIONS DE L'OCDE

ARGENTINA – ARGENTINE
Carlos Hirsch S.R.L.
Galería Güemes, Florida 165, 4° Piso
1333 Buenos Aires   Tel. (1) 331.1787 y 331.2391
Telefax: (1) 331.1787

AUSTRALIA – AUSTRALIE
D.A. Information Services
648 Whitehorse Road, P.O.B 163
Mitcham, Victoria 3132   Tel. (03) 873.4411
Telefax: (03) 873.5679

AUSTRIA – AUTRICHE
Gerold & Co.
Graben 31
Wien I   Tel. (0222) 533.50.14

BELGIUM – BELGIQUE
Jean De Lannoy
Avenue du Roi 202
B-1060 Bruxelles   Tel. (02) 538.51.69/538.08.41
Telefax: (02) 538.08.41

CANADA
Renouf Publishing Company Ltd.
1294 Algoma Road
Ottawa, ON K1B 3W8   Tel. (613) 741.4333
Telefax: (613) 741.5439
Stores:
61 Sparks Street
Ottawa, ON K1P 5R1   Tel. (613) 238.8985
211 Yonge Street
Toronto, ON M5B 1M4   Tel. (416) 363.3171
Telefax: (416)363.59.63
Les Éditions La Liberté Inc.
3020 Chemin Sainte-Foy
Sainte-Foy, PQ G1X 3V6   Tel. (418) 658.3763
Telefax: (418) 658.3763
Federal Publications Inc.
165 University Avenue, Suite 701
Toronto, ON M5H 3B8   Tel. (416) 860.1611
Telefax: (416) 860.1608
Les Publications Fédérales
1185 Université
Montréal, QC H3B 3A7   Tel. (514) 954.1633
Telefax : (514) 954.1635

CHINA – CHINE
China National Publications Import
Export Corporation (CNPIEC)
16 Gongti E. Road, Chaoyang District
P.O. Box 88 or 50
Beijing 100704 PR   Tel. (01) 506.6688
Telefax: (01) 506.3101

CZECH REPUBLIC – RÉPUBLIQUE TCHÈQUE
Artia Pegas Press Ltd.
Narodni Trida 25
POB 825
111 21 Praha 1   Tel. 26.65.68
Telefax: 26.20.81

DENMARK – DANEMARK
Munksgaard Book and Subscription Service
35, Nørre Søgade, P.O. Box 2148
DK-1016 København K   Tel. (33) 12.85.70
Telefax: (33) 12.93.87

EGYPT – ÉGYPTE
Middle East Observer
41 Sherif Street
Cairo   Tel. 392.6919
Telefax: 360-6804

FINLAND – FINLANDE
Akateeminen Kirjakauppa
Keskuskatu 1, P.O. Box 128
00100 Helsinki
Subscription Services/Agence d'abonnements :
P.O. Box 23
00371 Helsinki   Tel. (358 0) 12141
Telefax: (358 0) 121.4450

FRANCE
OECD/OCDE
Mail Orders/Commandes par correspondance:
2, rue André-Pascal
75775 Paris Cedex 16   Tel. (33-1) 45.24.82.00
Telefax: (33-1) 49.10.42.76
Telex: 640048 OCDE
Orders via Minitel, France only/
Commandes par Minitel, France exclusivement :
36 15 OCDE
OECD Bookshop/Librairie de l'OCDE :
33, rue Octave-Feuillet
75016 Paris   Tel. (33-1) 45.24.81.67
(33-1) 45.24.81.81
Documentation Française
29, quai Voltaire
75007 Paris   Tel. 40.15.70.00
Gibert Jeune (Droit-Économie)
6, place Saint-Michel
75006 Paris   Tel. 43.25.91.19
Librairie du Commerce International
10, avenue d'Iéna
75016 Paris   Tel. 40.73.34.60
Librairie Dunod
Université Paris-Dauphine
Place du Maréchal de Lattre de Tassigny
75016 Paris   Tel. (1) 44.05.40.13
Librairie Lavoisier
11, rue Lavoisier
75008 Paris   Tel. 42.65.39.95
Librairie L.G.D.J. - Montchrestien
20, rue Soufflot
75005 Paris   Tel. 46.33.89.85
Librairie des Sciences Politiques
30, rue Saint-Guillaume
75007 Paris   Tel. 45.48.36.02
P.U.F.
49, boulevard Saint-Michel
75005 Paris   Tel. 43.25.83.40
Librairie de l'Université
12a, rue Nazareth
13100 Aix-en-Provence   Tel. (16) 42.26.18.08
Documentation Française
165, rue Garibaldi
69003 Lyon   Tel. (16) 78.63.32.23
Librairie Decitre
29, place Bellecour
69002 Lyon   Tel. (16) 72.40.54.54

GERMANY – ALLEMAGNE
OECD Publications and Information Centre
August-Bebel-Allee 6
D-53175 Bonn   Tel. (0228) 959.120
Telefax: (0228) 959.12.17

GREECE – GRÈCE
Librairie Kauffmann
Mavrokordatou 9
106 78 Athens   Tel. (01) 32.55.321
Telefax: (01) 36.33.967

HONG-KONG
Swindon Book Co. Ltd.
13–15 Lock Road
Kowloon, Hong Kong   Tel. 2376.2062
Telefax: 2376.0685

HUNGARY – HONGRIE
Euro Info Service
Margitsziget, Európa Ház
1138 Budapest   Tel. (1) 111.62.16
Telefax : (1) 111.60.61

ICELAND – ISLANDE
Mál Mog Menning
Laugavegi 18, Pósthólf 392
121 Reykjavik   Tel. 162.35.23

INDIA – INDE
Oxford Book and Stationery Co.
Scindia House
New Delhi 110001   Tel.(11) 331.5896/5308
Telefax: (11) 332.5993
17 Park Street
Calcutta 700016   Tel. 240832

INDONESIA – INDONÉSIE
Pdii-Lipi
P.O. Box 4298
Jakarta 12042   Tel. (21) 573.34.67
Telefax: (21) 573.34.67

IRELAND – IRLANDE
Government Supplies Agency
Publications Section
4/5 Harcourt Road
Dublin 2   Tel. 661.31.11
Telefax: 478.06.45

ISRAEL
Praedicta
5 Shatner Street
P.O. Box 34030
Jerusalem 91430   Tel. (2) 52.84.90/1/2
Telefax: (2) 52.84.93
R.O.Y.
P.O. Box 13056
Tel Aviv 61130   Tél. (3) 49.61.08
Telefax (3) 544.60.39

ITALY – ITALIE
Libreria Commissionaria Sansoni
Via Duca di Calabria 1/1
50125 Firenze   Tel. (055) 64.54.15
Telefax: (055) 64.12.57
Via Bartolini 29
20155 Milano   Tel. (02) 36.50.83
Editrice e Libreria Herder
Piazza Montecitorio 120
00186 Roma   Tel. 679.46.28
Telefax: 678.47.51
Libreria Hoepli
Via Hoepli 5
20121 Milano   Tel. (02) 86.54.46
Telefax: (02) 805.28.86
Libreria Scientifica
Dott. Lucio de Biasio 'Aeiou'
Via Coronelli, 6
20146 Milano   Tel. (02) 48.95.45.52
Telefax: (02) 48.95.45.48

JAPAN – JAPON
OECD Publications and Information Centre
Landic Akasaka Building
2-3-4 Akasaka, Minato-ku
Tokyo 107   Tel. (81.3) 3586.2016
Telefax: (81.3) 3584.7929

KOREA – CORÉE
Kyobo Book Centre Co. Ltd.
P.O. Box 1658, Kwang Hwa Moon
Seoul   Tel. 730.78.91
Telefax: 735.00.30

MALAYSIA – MALAISIE
University of Malaya Bookshop
University of Malaya
P.O. Box 1127, Jalan Pantai Baru
59700 Kuala Lumpur
Malaysia   Tel. 756.5000/756.5425
Telefax: 756.3246

MEXICO – MEXIQUE
Revistas y Periodicos Internacionales S.A. de C.V.
Florencia 57 - 1004
Mexico, D.F. 06600   Tel. 207.81.00
Telefax : 208.39.79

NETHERLANDS - PAYS-BAS
SDU Uitgeverij Plantijnstraat
Externe Fondsen
Postbus 20014
2500 EA's-Gravenhage   Tel. (070) 37.89.880
Voor bestellingen: Telefax: (070) 34.75.778

NEW ZEALAND
NOUVELLE-ZÉLANDE
Legislation Services
P.O. Box 12418
Thorndon, Wellington   Tel. (04) 496.5652
                              Telefax: (04) 496.5698

NORWAY - NORVÈGE
Narvesen Info Center - NIC
Bertrand Narvesens vei 2
P.O. Box 6125 Etterstad
0602 Oslo 6   Tel. (022) 57.33.00
                     Telefax: (022) 68.19.01

PAKISTAN
Mirza Book Agency
65 Shahrah Quaid-E-Azam
Lahore 54000   Tel. (42) 353.601
                      Telefax: (42) 231.730

PHILIPPINE - PHILIPPINES
International Book Center
5th Floor, Filipinas Life Bldg.
Ayala Avenue
Metro Manila   Tel. 81.96.76
                      Telex 23312 RHP PH

PORTUGAL
Livraria Portugal
Rua do Carmo 70-74
Apart. 2681
1200 Lisboa   Tel.: (01) 347.49.82/5
                     Telefax: (01) 347.02.64

SINGAPORE - SINGAPOUR
Gower Asia Pacific Pte Ltd.
Golden Wheel Building
41, Kallang Pudding Road, No. 04-03
Singapore 1334   Tel. 741.5166
                        Telefax: 742.9356

SPAIN - ESPAGNE
Mundi-Prensa Libros S.A.
Castelló 37, Apartado 1223
Madrid 28001   Tel. (91) 431.33.99
                      Telefax: (91) 575.39.98

Libreria Internacional AEDOS
Consejo de Ciento 391
08009 - Barcelona   Tel. (93) 488.30.09
                           Telefax: (93) 487.76.59
Llibreria de la Generalitat
Palau Moja
Rambla dels Estudis, 118
08002 - Barcelona
          (Subscripcions) Tel. (93) 318.80.12
          (Publicacions) Tel. (93) 302.67.23
                         Telefax: (93) 412.18.54

SRI LANKA
Centre for Policy Research
c/o Colombo Agencies Ltd.
No. 300-304, Galle Road
Colombo 3   Tel. (1) 574240, 573551-2
                   Telefax: (1) 575394, 510711

SWEDEN - SUÈDE
Fritzes Information Center
Box 16356
Regeringsgatan 12
106 47 Stockholm   Tel. (08) 690.90.90
                          Telefax: (08) 20.50.21

Subscription Agency/Agence d'abonnements :
Wennergren-Williams Info AB
P.O. Box 1305
171 25 Solna   Tel. (08) 705.97.50
                      Téléfax : (08) 27.00.71

SWITZERLAND - SUISSE
Maditec S.A. (Books and Periodicals - Livres
et périodiques)
Chemin des Palettes 4
Case postale 266
1020 Renens VD 1   Tel. (021) 635.08.65
                          Telefax: (021) 635.07.80

Librairie Payot S.A.
4, place Pépinet
CP 3212
1002 Lausanne   Tel. (021) 341.33.47
                       Telefax: (021) 341.33.45

Librairie Unilivres
6, rue de Candolle
1205 Genève   Tel. (022) 320.26.23
                     Telefax: (022) 329.73.18

Subscription Agency/Agence d'abonnements :
Dynapresse Marketing S.A.
38 avenue Vibert
1227 Carouge   Tel.: (022) 308.07.89
                      Telefax : (022) 308.07.99

See also - Voir aussi :
OECD Publications and Information Centre
August-Bebel-Allee 6
D-53175 Bonn (Germany)   Tel. (0228) 959.120
                                Telefax: (0228) 959.12.17

TAIWAN - FORMOSE
Good Faith Worldwide Int'l. Co. Ltd.
9th Floor, No. 118, Sec. 2
Chung Hsiao E. Road
Taipei   Tel. (02) 391.7396/391.7397
                Telefax: (02) 394.9176

THAILAND - THAÏLANDE
Suksit Siam Co. Ltd.
113, 115 Fuang Nakhon Rd.
Opp. Wat Rajbopith
Bangkok 10200   Tel. (662) 225.9531/2
                       Telefax: (662) 222.5188

TURKEY - TURQUIE
Kültür Yayinlari Is-Türk Ltd. Sti.
Atatürk Bulvari No. 191/Kat 13
Kavaklidere/Ankara   Tel. 428.11.40 Ext. 2458
Dolmabahce Cad. No. 29
Besiktas/Istanbul   Tel. 260.71.88
                           Telex: 43482B

UNITED KINGDOM - ROYAUME-UNI
HMSO
Gen. enquiries   Tel. (071) 873 0011
Postal orders only:
P.O. Box 276, London SW8 5DT
Personal Callers HMSO Bookshop
49 High Holborn, London WC1V 6HB
                       Telefax: (071) 873 8200
Branches at: Belfast, Birmingham, Bristol, Edin-
burgh, Manchester

UNITED STATES - ÉTATS-UNIS
OECD Publications and Information Centre
2001 L Street N.W., Suite 700
Washington, D.C. 20036-4910 Tel. (202) 785.6323
                            Telefax: (202) 785.0350

VENEZUELA
Libreria del Este
Avda F. Miranda 52, Aptdo. 60337
Edificio Galipán
Caracas 106   Tel. 951.1705/951.2307/951.1297
                     Telegram: Libreste Caracas

Subscription to OECD periodicals may also be
placed through main subscription agencies.

Les abonnements aux publications périodiques de
l'OCDE peuvent être souscrits auprès des
principales agences d'abonnement.

Orders and inquiries from countries where Distribu-
tors have not yet been appointed should be sent to:
OECD Publications Service, 2 rue André-Pascal,
75775 Paris Cedex 16, France.

Les commandes provenant de pays où l'OCDE n'a
pas encore désigné de distributeur peuvent être
adressées à : OCDE, Service des Publications,
2, rue André-Pascal, 75775 Paris Cedex 16, France.

1-1995

OECD PUBLICATIONS, 2 rue André-Pascal, 75775 PARIS CEDEX 16
PRINTED IN FRANCE
(95 95 01 1) ISBN 92-64-14324-6 - No. 47661 1995